THAT IS A GOOD IDEA

IDEAS TO MAKE MONEY DURING THESE TIMES OF COVID

HERBERT KING

CONTENTS

INTRODUCTION

Since the beginning of COVID-19, many people around the world have had to resort to working from home during lockdowns, or have lost their jobs and needed to find ways to make an income when they weren't able to leave their homes. COVID has proved to be fairly costly—for both individuals and economies. With each passing hour, this virus has cost global economies millions and millions of dollars, with more businesses being forced to close and workers beginning to rely on disaster relief payments or grants to get by.

Many have found themselves depending on side-hustles to pay their bills. With the abrupt closure of many businesses, COVID-19 has actually started to usher in a new era of remote work for millions of people around the world. It's proven that we can make money without having to physically make it to work. It's opened up a plethora of pathways to other careers and sources of passive income. Basically, COVID has become a massive work-from-home experiment that has given us insight into different ways we can make an income from our homes, or even just simply social-distancing ourselves during the pandemic.

You've probably been going a bit stir-crazy while sitting around at home. Maybe you've picked up a hobby you never had time for before or found a new one to fill in the empty hours of lazing around the house. Have you considered, though, that these hobbies and interests could potentially turn into passive income during these times of lockdown? That you could do something you truly enjoy instead of slaving away at a job you simply keep out of need. COVID has pushed a lot of people into a state of instability—but that doesn't mean you can't turn things around.

This book will touch on just a few different ways you'll be able to make active and passive income—all while following the guidelines of lockdown. We'll discuss small, and sometimes unconventional ways, where you can make a few extra dollars. Plus, with most people finding that they have too much time on their hands while being stuck at home, you can use that extra time to make some cash while you wait for your life to get back to normal.

From teaching online to creating affiliated blogs and websites, writing books, and creating podcasts, I'll share with you some ways that you can dive into to make that extra money you might need or want. With in-depth how-to's, you'll be ready to start your new hobby or side hustle in no time. Or, you could even turn some of these ideas into full-fledged careers—something you might not have considered before.

Whatever your aim is for reading this book, you can be sure to find information that will help assist you in these hard times. I hope this book will be able to give you the push you need to try out something new, or perhaps give you the motivation to get into something you've always wanted to do in the first place. Or, at least it can give you some good ideas to use as a basis for something else you might enjoy.

Don't let COVID-19 bring you down. It's time to get back to work, but this time, it's time to do what you enjoy doing while making some money.

1

TEACHING ONLINE

WHILE TEACHING itself isn't a new concept, teaching online, and to students halfway around the world in just a few minutes, is. Tutoring has been a good source of income for many students throughout their high school and university years, but now it's also becoming a great resource for adults as well. Some would even consider themselves full-time online teachers, making enough money to support themselves solely through online teaching platforms. And, due to the COVID-19 pandemic, teaching online has become more prevalent than ever before.

As this demand for online learning increases, so is the demand for online teachers. However, the number of people applying for this type of freelancing work is comparatively quite low. So, for those who believe they have something to offer in terms of teaching and need to earn a living while sitting at home, online tutoring just might be your answer. Besides making a decent amount of money, it can open up a plethora of learning opportunities as well. It's entirely a give-and-take process, where you'll learn just as much from your students as they do from you.

There are two different types of online teaching; tutoring in specific subjects or categories, and English as a Second Language (ESL). One is much more relaxed than the other, with far fewer requirements, but we'll go over both just in case. When it comes to online tutoring, you won't need any fancy certification, but you will need to exhibit solid knowledge of the subjects you'll be teaching. Luckily, there are various different subjects that could be taught—from business English to writing resumes, from science to history. You can simply use your own work experience or career field to teach in a specific subject.

For example, one company called Chegg is an online platform where individuals are hired as subject matter experts. You can apply if you believe you're good at any specific subject such as commerce or art. These experts are hired to answer questions from students all over the world and the expert is paid based on the number of these answers. The payment is entirely based on your performance.

ESL, on the other hand, does require more. For example, many online-learning companies work with countries that require teachers to at least have a bachelor's degree along with teaching certifications. Luckily, these certifications aren't too difficult to obtain and could be beneficial if you'd ever want to take your teaching career overseas.

Why Online Teaching Jobs Might Be Right For You

These jobs are perfect for those who love to learn and grow. You'll have chances to expand your horizons, possibly interacting with students from all over the world, plus you'll be keeping in touch with the subject of your interest.

Nowadays, online teaching has become a blessing, especially as this virus has most places shutting down. Teaching online provides a decent income for those wishing to work from home and avoid going out during this time. It's also a great way to meet other people with diverse backgrounds, and to socialize online while making some money.

These types of jobs are also super flexible, with online teaching portals providing time slots throughout the day where you can pick and choose your hours. You can work for as many hours as you'd like, in the morning or afternoon. You can choose whatever time is most convenient for you, though different times will come with more or fewer bookings due to students living in various time zones.

Another great thing about teaching online, and why it might be the best option for you, is that you can earn money based on an hourly premise. Bigger companies either pay in dollars or pounds and directly deposit your paycheck to your bank account. This could be on a week-by-week basis, or monthly. Either way, it's a good way to make a steady income if you build up your teaching platform and have regular students.

What You'll Need

As I noted above, there are different qualifications when it comes to the two main areas of teaching online. If you're leaning towards more relaxed tutoring positions, the most important thing you'll need is knowledge on the subject you'll be covering. Yet, if you're hoping to go down the ESL path, you'll need just a bit more qualifications. We'll go over the requirements for both types of teaching.

For online tutoring, all you really need is a working computer and reliable Wi-Fi. Many teaching platforms will test the speed and reliability of your internet connection, but once you've passed, you're basically good to go. It might help to create a fun and interesting learning background for students, but it's not always necessary. When applying for online teaching platforms, be sure to check out the requirements they have for hiring new tutors or teachers.

As for ESL, that's a different matter. While having a good computer and reliable Internet is a must, many ESL companies will require more. For example, some will require that the teacher is a native-English speaker with a bachelor's degree and some sort of ESL certification such as the TEFL, TESOL, or CELTA.

Though there are some online teaching companies that don't require you to be a native-English speaker, it would be better for you to have a firm grasp on the language, as it is the main language used to teach online unless you're teaching another language. In fact, many companies will even base your rate on your English level if you're teaching broader subjects—much like how language teaching companies would base your pay on your level of any specific language other than English.

While you won't always need to have a degree in the field you're wanting to teach with both online tutoring and ESL teaching, it would still be better for you to have some sort of university degree. The majority of companies will only require proof of at least a bachelor's degree in any field. Which means you're not usually required to have a degree in either English or education. There are some companies that accept teachers without a bachelor's degree, but those are rare and might not be as reliable when it comes to taking care of their teachers or pay.

Before you become an ESL teacher, you'll usually be required to complete a 120-hour TEFL or TESOL certification that is internationally recognized or comes from a reliable institution. While these certifications vary in price and can be done online, you must make sure you're getting this certification from a reputable company. We'll go into these types of certifications and how to get them more in-depth in the next section.

Another difference between simple online tutoring and ESL teaching is that you'll need a proper space to conduct your classes. Whereas online tutoring companies might not require anything from you other than a plain, white background and good lighting, ESL companies will most likely want you to decorate your background. They might also require you to use realia, or physical objects to assist you in your lessons such as vocabulary cards, or stuffed animals if you teach children. These companies will also be checking to see if you have adequate lighting and are dressed professionally.

ESL Certifications: What They Are & How To Get Them

If you're wanting to go the ESL route with online teaching, the first step would be getting certified. There are a few different types of ESL certifications and many different institutions that offer them, but not all are accredited. It is insanely important to make sure that your ESL certification comes from an accredited institution. For example, the International TEFL Academy is internationally recognized and is accepted by online companies from all over the world. This institution also offers support in assisting their alumni in finding ESL teaching jobs, with information on different countries if they'd ever like to move overseas.

These certifications will often take about two to five months to complete, with online lessons that can be done at any given time within that period. After you complete the lessons at your own pace, you'll be required to complete a type of practicum. Usually, this can be done at your local community center, aiding already certified teachers in ESL classrooms there, or you can gain practicum experience from other courses that provide practicum hours online and give you recorded class sessions to add to your portfolio.

The best thing about being certified in teaching English as a second language isn't just gaining a new job or a diploma, but the experience itself is also gratifying. Having these certifications will give you

that extra boost you need to be seen as a working professional—
even if you're simply tutoring online and not teaching English in
more professional online settings.

But first, you need to make sure you're actually choosing the right
certification. There are about eight different types, all of which
provide different educational experiences and open different doors
for your teaching career.

TOEFL is the acronym for 'Test of English as a Foreign Language'.
This certification is popular in the USA or in other countries where
English is more commonly taught or spoken.

TESOL is short for Teaching English to Speakers of Other
Languages. This certification has various levels where you can
choose to do a longer or shorter course according to your previous
experience in teaching or your needs. It can be used to work with
both non-native and native-English speaking countries and can also
help prepare you to teach business English or immigrants.

TEFL, or Teaching English as a Foreign Language, is one of the more
common certifications, along with TESOL, though this one is more
popular in the United Kingdom. This certification is generally
accepted around the world and is used mainly for teaching non-
native English-speaking countries.

CELTA stands for Certificate for English Language Teaching to
Adults and, as the name suggests, is mainly needed to teach...well,
adults. It's a more advanced qualification from the University of
Cambridge and is required by global institutions like the British
Council. This type of certification is also needed to teach abroad in
Europe if you'd like to do that someday after Covid-19.

While I only covered just four of the eight different certifications, I
would highly suggest researching the other ones if you're interested
in this career path. These four are the most popular certifications,
especially when it comes to teaching online, with most companies

preferring the TEFL or TESOL. And, while obtaining one of these isn't always necessary for tutoring online, especially in other subjects, it might just be handy due to the fact that they teach you how to be a successful teacher, both online and in a classroom.

Online Teaching Companies

When looking for the right online teaching platform, it's best to do your research. You'll want to find a teaching company that not only pays you well but is also a reputable company. There are a ton of different online teaching companies, some that have been around for years, while others are just now popping up. Each online teaching company and platform caters to different teachers and students, so be sure to choose the right fit for your qualifications and needs.

Many online teaching companies cater towards ESL teaching for Chinese, Taiwanese, or Japanese students, though some platforms are open-tutoring platforms. Some of the most well-known ESL companies are iTutorgroup, Tutor ABC, and VIPKid. Other language-focused platforms include italki and Cambly. There are also many different tutoring platforms such as Outschool, Care.com, and PrepNow Tutoring.

ESL companies such as iTutorgroup and VIPKid require at least a bachelor's degree and an ESL certificate. These companies also require you to be a native-English speaker and prefer for you to have some sort of ESL teaching experience, though it isn't required. ITutorgroup caters to both children and adults, while VIPKid mainly focuses on children ages 4-12 from China. These companies provide pre-designed lessons for you already, along with giving you extra support, such as giving tips on how to conduct the lesson while teaching it. However, as their main base are children and adults from China, Taiwan, and Japan, teachers from North America might be up late or have to work insanely early in the morning to book lessons.

Whereas some ESL companies will provide you with in-depth lesson plans, most do not. For example, if you want to work at Cambly, you'll be expected to provide your lessons, mostly centered around conversational English. Teaching for companies like Cambly can both be easier and harder than other ESL companies. Most of your students here will expect and request conversation lessons, rather than lecture or activity-based ones. You'll need to be able to drive the conversation at various English levels and be ready to keep the energy and conversation flowing.

Italki is a similar platform that connects students to fluent speakers but doesn't just focus on English. This site allows students to find teachers in any language they want to learn—so you don't actually have to be a native-English speaker to teach with them. If your professional background is in languages, or maybe you're just bilingual, this would be a great opportunity for you to make some money.

Whereas Cambly, iTutorgroup, and italki focus on languages, other sites such as Outschool are more tutor-based. Though most teachers on this platform use it to give multi-student courses, you can offer tutoring services there as well. You can create a class on any subject you feel you know the most, such as history or even cooking classes. The only downside is that, unlike other platforms, you aren't given a curriculum to follow and will have a lesson plan for your students. And, while it's free to post your courses, Outschool does take a 30% fee from any payment you earn on commission.

Care.com is another trusted tutoring site where parents can look up tutors, as well as babysitters or nannies. This company requires an ID and a background check, so parents feel safer. Once you're cleared, however, you'll be able to create a profile and offer your own tutoring services online for whatever rates you want. While this isn't an actual teaching platform, you can always use Skype or Zoom to conduct your online classes. However, if you're wanting to actually find clients through this site, you'll need to pay the monthly premium membership fee—though it's not too bad considering Care.com doesn't require a commission fee.

PrepNow Tutoring is another tutoring site that focuses on ACT/SAT Test Prep and Advanced Mathematics. Their test prep curriculum is ready for you to use, and they will even guide you on how to use their curriculum. You can set your own hours, and it's a good option for those who are able to teach this subject and are new to the tutoring game.

If you're not feeling any of these options, you can always try to build your own student base and simply conduct tutoring sessions through Zoom or Skype, as I mentioned above. These companies just happen to give you an already-made student base to build from, though you can always try and build your own.

Whatever you decide to do, just be sure to conduct your own research to avoid being scammed or lose your money. Teaching online can be a great income source, and it's not too difficult to get into.

After Covid

Teaching online isn't just a great source of income while being stuck inside—it could open so many doors for you in the future. One big aspect of online teaching is flexibility. As long as you have a good laptop and wifi, you can take this job just about anywhere.

Many people have actually done just that.

If you plan on taking my advice on getting a teaching certificate, such as a TEFL or CELTA, you don't have to limit yourself. These certificates will open new doors to you where you could actually teach abroad, away from your home country. Many non-English speaking countries such as China, Egypt, Brazil, and more actively seek out native English speakers with these certificates to teach in their schools. Some might not even require a teaching certificate.

If you love to travel, this could be the perfect opportunity for you. This side hustle you picked up simply for the sake of making extra money during COVID could actually propel you into the world of teaching English abroad. And, if you find yourself in countries where the American dollar goes a long way, you could actually make a good living from it as well.

Teaching online will not only give you the flexibility and extra cash you might need now, but it could also give you the tools you can use in the future when COVID has eased up and travel becomes normal once again. You can pack your bags—making sure to take your laptop with you—and set off on adventures around the world, using your online teaching as a way to make an income while doing so.

Many people have taken up this call across the globe, with some native English speakers actually making new lives in foreign countries. So, as you can see, you aren't just limited to being stuck at home, going through the same motions day after day. This is one of the few ideas in this book that could lead to more—more career paths, more opportunities, and overall, more flexibility.

If you want to learn more about how you can take your online teaching further, many of the teaching certificate institutions mentioned above will have amazing resources you can use and utilize. Or, you can check out Dave's ESL Cafe, a website where schools and other education institutions post job listings for both qualified and uncertified native English speakers to come work and teach for them.

The world can become yours, and all from something you picked up while in lockdown during COVID-19.

2

AFFILIATE PROGRAMS

WITH THE RISE of the pandemic, many people have turned to online work to make some extra cash. The number of blogs, vlogs, and websites have increased since lock-down, leaving a lot of people with some extra time on their hands. And, one great way to make some passive income is to turn your website into an affiliate site. The easiest way to monetize your site is to start a blog.

If you don't know what blogging is already, it's a dairy-style website or page that regularly updates readers on specific topics or about the writer's everyday life. It's one way many promote their side businesses such as photography or traveling, and has boosted influencers online for years now.

Yet, blogging can be more than just simply logging your emotions or thoughts. You can make some passive income off of it as well. If you're a blogger looking to monetize your personal website, or looking to start one just to increase your passive income, you need to check out affiliate marketing. It's a win-win strategy for writers, bloggers, vloggers, or basically anyone with any sort of web presence that has good traffic.

Affiliate, or associate programs, are casual arrangements made between an online business and the person who owns the website. The blogger, or web owner, sends their readers or viewers to the online business, giving them what we call traffic. In return, that business gives the blogger a commission.

It seems easy enough, right? But there's more to affiliate programs than simply posting a link to your websites. Not only are there different kinds of affiliate programs, but there are also different commission rates, Clickbank gravity, earnings per click, and a whole thing about website cookies. It can get a bit confusing if you don't understand what affiliate programs are or how you can best utilize them.

But don't worry, that's what I'm here for.

How They Work

It's remarkably easy to start a blog these days if you haven't already. All you need is a computer and a website. If you're a business owner and already own your own site, simply adding a blog page is no problem. It's a great way to engage your customers and to create some foot traffic to your website. When your readers come to your blog for their weekly or monthly updates or find your website through the search engine, they'll also be able to see your affiliate links.

But how, exactly, do affiliate links work?

When it comes to affiliate programs, there are three parties: the customer (your reader), the affiliate site (your blog), and the merchant site. Over the past few years, affiliate programs have been on the rise—and for a great reason. It allows websites that don't partake in e-commerce to still participate and earn money online. There are three main types of affiliate program payment options: pay-per-sale, pay-per-click, and pay-per-lead. Each comes with its own benefits, depending on your website and what you do.

Pay-per-sale is exactly how it sounds. The online business will pay an affiliate when they send them a customer who actually buys something. Some merchant sites like Amazon.com pay the affiliate a percentage of the sale, sort of like a commission. Others pay a fixed amount. It all depends on their terms of agreement with the affiliate website.

Pay-per-click is when the merchant pays the affiliate based on the number of viewers that click on the link leading to the merchant website. You don't need to worry about them actually buying anything, simply clicking on the link is good enough.

Finally, pay-per-lead means an affiliate gets paid once their viewer signs up for a service or contact from the merchant website. The visitor will fill out some type of requested information which the merchant might use as a lead or sell to another company for a lead.

While there are a number of other agreements and different ways to get paid, these are the main three. A company will basically set up an affiliate program that benefits them based on any actions they need taken on their website. Then they simply pay the affiliate for that action taken by those viewers.

It sounds simple enough, right? But that's the basic overview of affiliate links. It's time to dig much deeper.

Starting a Blog

If you've got the spare time, and are ready to make the leap into blogging, then you'll first want to figure out what, exactly, you want to blog about. What are some of your hobbies or interests? Are you really passionate about a certain field or topic? Maybe you just simply want to use your blog as a journal, sharing your life with the world. Whatever it is you want to blog about, you'll need to be able to come up with engaging and interesting content to pull in readers.

The first thing readers will see is your blog's name. You'll want to pick one that will generally hint at the topics you'll be writing about, or if you're trying to create a brand—choose that as the name. You can even simply just use your own name for the title.

Your blog's niche will be the topic area you'll be focusing your content around, and if you plan on making some passive income from it, you might be correlating your blog content with whatever affiliate niche you'd like to promote. This could be topics related to travel, food, fashion, technology, gaming, or even lifestyle. Try using some of the words that correlate to your niche in the name of your blog.

Once you have an idea of what you'll want to blog about and have a name for it, you'll want to take the next step: finding the best web hosting site. This is where you'll actually get your blog online. A website host is where you'll keep all your online files safe and secure, and it also allows other people to actually access your blog. Think of web hosting as a sort of home where people will be able to come to see what's inside when they type in your blog's URL.

There are various different web hosting companies, all with different subscriptions and costs. One of the easiest is Wix or Squarespace. These come with templates that will allow you to easily design and edit your website or blog page. They're fairly affordable as well. If you're wanting to go all out, and find a more professional host site, you could check out Bluehost. Bluehost is more expensive, but it's perfect for those in creative fields as it allows better quality for photos and videos. Bluehost, however, is just a host. You can link your Bluehost accounts to other platforms such as WordPress, which is both a hosting site and website creator. WordPress also has its own subscriptions, like Wix or Squarespace. All of these sites will also allow you to purchase your own domain name—just to seem a bit more professional rather than going with the free options.

Which is how we come to the next step: choosing your domain name. As I mentioned, websites will offer free domain names, but they'll be linked to that site such as .wordpress.com or .wix.com. If you want to seem more legitimate, these websites offer plans that will allow you to have a free domain of your choice for up to a year. After that, most domains only cost between $4-$12 per year. Luckily, they're fairly cheap.

Once you have taken all the necessary steps to create your website, you can either design the pages yourself or hire a professional. Then, all you have to do is upload and create your content. You can use this content to generate income by using the affiliate links, which we will discuss more in-depth below.

Revenue Share

A revenue share, also called a 'Revshare,' is a model that's followed by some affiliate programs where the affiliate gets a commission for the total sales of a referral. This is a great model for affiliates who are looking to build long-term business relationships with the retailers of the services or products they promote.

This pay-per-sale has become a highly effective payment model. Instead of paying a fixed amount to the affiliate, the merchant will pay a percentage of the total sale amount. Top brands like Airbnb and Reebok have switched over to this type of payment model as it's a more cost-effective way for them to build their business.

For example, if a merchant is offering a specific commission, let's say about 30%, and a viewer from your website buys a product from them that equals $1,000, you'll get $300 in return. As their affiliate, you'd be entitled to a percentage of that profit, and the best part? These types of arrangements are usually for a lifetime. Or, at least as long as you send traffic to that merchant site through your own website.

This all sounds great, but how do you know if revenue share, or pay-per-sale, is right for you? Well, if your leads are consistent and active, this would be a great option. This type of model has a huge potential to earn you some money, but you'll need to consider how active your viewers are. Will they be loyal to the brand you're promoting, or make repeat purchases? This is something you need to think about before you dive into this type of model.

Cost Per Click

Cost-per-click, or pay-per-click, is another type of model where the affiliate gets paid when a viewer clicks on a link. This is a highly scalable commission model specifically used in performance marketing. Top brands use this model to increase their own traffic, attract more viewers, or generate high-quality leads and sales.

If you're an affiliate marketer, all you have to do is post the link to your website, advertising whatever company or product you'd like, and wait for your viewers to click on that banner, button, or text. You'll either be offered a flat fee or a percentage based on commission.

This model is highly measurable as you can calculate just how much you'll earn using your own data from your website to keep track of the number of clicks. It's highly recommended for websites that already have an audience that has a basic understanding of the products or services being promoted. Yet, even if you're new to affiliate marketing, CPC offers you an easy way to track your earnings and beginners can apply for even the most seasoned affiliate programs. However, you'll need to have a basic grasp of targeting your audience to help increase your income.

Cost Per Lead

This type of affiliate marketing payment model is when you get paid for any sign-ups your viewers do on the merchant's site. The merchant will accept a lead or certain action from a potential customer that can be used for their own marketing needs. Though the pay is lower than the revenue share model, there's also a lower amount of risk.

Typically, as the affiliate, you'd need to somehow convince your viewers to give basic information through the merchant's online form to get paid. If your viewer clicks on your referral link and decides to take any action on the merchant's site such as filling out a contact form, downloading an e-book or an app, then that viewer becomes what we call a lead. Merchants use this lead to advertise to the viewer in the future.

For each lead, you'll most likely get a fixed amount as a commission. But, remember, your viewer will have to submit basic contact information which many might not want to do. So, while this model is typically low-risk, it might also be more difficult to earn an income. Those who succeed with this type of model will usually have viewers who are interested in taking some sort of action for a product or service.

Cost Per Action

Unlike the other models, cost-per-action is pretty straightforward, and it's different from a cost-per-lead. Whereas you get paid for each lead you generate for the merchant in CPL, for CPA your viewer won't have to submit any information. Instead, you'll be paid a one-time fee once a sale is generated. This is also different from revenue share models where you get paid each time your viewers renew a plan or make a repeat purchase.

It can be a lucrative opportunity for affiliates who have just started out, or for those with a little more experience. But, while it's still a low-risk and highly scalable model, you'll still need to make sure you have the right audience for it and this type of model can have some fierce competition. And, although you technically don't have to invest your own money to make this model work, many start out with a minimum of $1500 US dollars to improve the speed of their landing page. Some might also outsource their content development and website design work to professionals to make their advertisements more clickable to their viewers.

Cost Per Mile

Finally, we have the cost-per-mile model. In this model, the merchants will usually pay a fixed rate for a certain amount of impressions or views. You'll be paid when your advertisement is shown a certain amount of times, usually a thousand at least. What's great about this model is that you'll be paid whether or not your viewers click on this ad.

All you need to do is make your advertisement on your website or blog as appealing as possible. It's ideal for those who have a sizable audience or have high traffic through their site. For merchants, however, this is a high-risk model, so it isn't always used. For the merchants, they'll have to pay you regardless of whether your viewers buy something or take action.

Verticals

If you're wanting to branch out into affiliate marketing, you'll not only need to understand the payment models but also what a vertical is. By understanding affiliate marketing verticals, you'll know what your target demographics will be and the best way to collect information about these demographics before getting started.

A vertical in the affiliate marketing world are markets that encompass a group of businesses. These verticals usually target one specific niche and are in-tuned with the special needs of these target demographics. And, although there are some businesses that can fall beneath two or more verticals, these companies don't usually cater to broader markets.

For example, if you're a travel blogger who wants to monetize their website, you'll most likely want to look for affiliate programs under the travel vertical. It's one of the most popular affiliation verticals as the travel market is highly profitable. Or, if you're a fashion website, try checking out the fashion affiliate programs. This niche is expected to become three times bigger than what it is now, especially with online shopping becoming more popular. Or maybe you're a gamer with your own YouTube channel. Streaming your games could attract gaming fans and you could earn a decent amount of money from any gaming affiliate program.

There are tons of different niches you could specialize in or look into before starting your website or blog. There are verticals in almost every market; technology, automotive, makeup, pet, health, education, sports, dating, and even cryptocurrency. The traits that define each demographic can be found in the way certain people utilize the internet, showing their interests, or products they buy online.

So, how do you choose the best vertical? Obviously, not everyone will be your target demographic. You need to choose products and services that will interest your audience in a way that also reflects your online presence. So, for example, if you're into gaming, and have an entire YouTube channel about that topic, you wouldn't be setting up advertisements for pet products. Unless those pet products are Mario and Luigi costumes.

However, you should also try to choose a niche that's easily expandable. Take the makeup niche; you could be an expert on hair products, which could then lead to skin and nail products as well. This could help to expand your reach and your passive income.

Best Affiliate Programs

Choosing the best affiliate program is a must when looking into monetizing your blog or website. You'll need to find one that fits the payment model you're looking for, as well as a correlating niche that fits your online presence. Here are some of the best affiliate programs to help get you started.

For Bloggers

Rakuten Marketing has a top-ranked affiliate program for bloggers. With more than 1 million merchants, you'll be able to find products from huge corporations such as Sephora, LEGO, Microsoft, and more to fit the vertical you're looking for. With a simple interface and amazing support, this program is great for those just starting out.

Another great program would be the CJ Affiliate. Their interface is also easy to navigate, and the advertisement filters will allow you to identify the best programs for you. It also has a widget creator for your website that will allow you to drag-and-drop the products you want to advertise into a slideshow, grid, or collage. With companies such as Barnes & Noble, Travelocity, Lowe's, and others, you'll have no problem finding a program that fits your needs.

ShareASale has over four thousand merchants, with some paying up to $300 for every sale made, though it doesn't have the same high-brand companies that Rakuten or CJ has. Still, they have amazing search parameters and have a two-tier program filter to show you which products will help you earn a better commission for your referrals.

Creative Market is another great affiliate program—especially if you're looking for a niche. This program specializes in photos, graphics, and WordPress themes, so if your audience is looking to build their own websites or blogs, this would be a great option.

Final Words

Whatever affiliate program you choose, be sure to research their terms and their niche. Affiliate programs work on trust between the customer, affiliate, and the merchant, so be sure to choose a product or service that you feel comfortable promoting. To become an affiliate, all you need to do is find the affiliate network, apply, and wait for their approval. Once they approve your application, you can begin looking for the right program that fits your niche and your needs. When a merchant accepts you, all you'll need to then is keep working on your website's content and wait for the money to roll right in.

3

PET CARE AFFILIATE

IF YOU'RE STRUGGLING to come up with an idea on what affiliate program you'd like to take part in, or have no idea what type of niche you'd like to monetize, pet affiliates are always a great idea. The pet vertical is one that has a lot of fans and a personal appeal. Any pet lover would spend money to care for and provide the best products for their furry little friends. And, in the United States alone, about $72 billion is spent on pet products per year, with $31 billion spent on pet food and treats, $16 billion spent on pet supplies, $18 billion spent on veterinary care, and $7 billion spent on other pet purchases.

Pet affiliate programs are a lucrative option—especially for those who are pet owners or love animals anyway. This industry is already big and still growing. With thousands of top brand companies and high-quality products, there are so many options for you to choose from. From GPS collars to holistic pet medicine, you'll easily be able to find a niche that's perfect for you. As an affiliate, you could find more than a few different ways to earn an income by joining one of these programs.

To start, if you haven't already, all you need is a website related to anything about pets or animals. Whether it's a blog dedicated to cute birds, easy-going fish, or all-natural pet care products, it would perfectly fit this vertical's niche. Plus, making money from this vertical is actually quite easy considering all the pet product merchants work with the top affiliate networks or have their own in-house affiliate programs.

If you're wanting to assist pet owners in finding the best products for their fur baby or have some great content ideas related to animals, then here's a comprehensive list of pet affiliate programs.

Hepper

Hepper is a cat product company that provides high-quality products such as beds, pods, and scratchers. It's also one of the best affiliate programs to work within the pet vertical. Their program is a cost-per-sale model where you can make an 8%-10% commission monthly. This company is constantly seeking to better its program by revising its products and listening to feedback from professionals. They also work with veterinarians who help ensure the quality of their products, which makes them trustworthy.

Petco Supplies

You've probably heard of this company if you've ever owned a pet before, but you might not have known about their affiliate program. Besides selling basically everything a pet owner could possibly need, this company also offers dog grooming services, veterinarian services, obedience classes, and even pet sitting. Their affiliate payment model is cost-per-click, which is extremely high. You could earn up to $45 per click.

Pet Heaven

Pet Heaven is a South African online pet product company that sells everything from food to toys and accessories. It's actually one of the leading brands of pet care products in South Africa. Through their affiliate program, you'd be able to log in to check your performance with their data of traffic, commission, and sales at any time—which could be super helpful in tracking your income. They also give you a wide range of creative banners and links that are ready for you to use on your website. This program is based on the pay-for-sale model where you can earn up to $6 for first-time sales.

Ollie

Ollie is a dog food brand that is set apart from other dog food companies. Not only do they make meals from human-grade meat, ensuring the quality of the food for your dog, but they also make tailor-made diets depending on your dog's breed, age, and activity levels. They also offer some of the best numbers when it comes to their affiliates. Any clients that are referred through your affiliate link give you an automatic $60 commission. It has both a pay-per-sale and pay-per-click payment model. Plus, this company donates part of their process to dogs in need—what more could you ask for?

PetPlate

PetPlate is another human-quality dog food company that provides a subscription service. Their food is created by pet nutritionists and cooked by a team of chefs, providing as little processing as possible and using USDA-approved meat, fruits, and vegetables. The prepackaged food is delivered straight to the clients, making it easy, and they operate primarily in the United States. However, if you're wanting to join their affiliate program, you'll need to be a member of either Share a Sale or become a member of their in-house program.

If you do become an affiliate for them, you could make a pretty good commission at 25%.

Paw.Com

Paw.Com specializes in pet beds, some of the best in the industry. Their beds are unique in the way that you can match them to your house's decor. They also come as throwaway rugs, which could be the ultimate comfort for any pet. These beds are made with memory foam, complete with replaceable and odor-resistant covers. This company offers a bit lower commission rates than others, but they give a pretty decent amount of earnings per click.

Chewy

Chewy is a pay-per-action affiliate program that provides various different products for cats, dogs, and other pets such as reptiles, birds, and horses. They have huge market affiliates to choose from— more than a thousand, actually. Their affiliate program is through Partnerize where affiliates will make a flat fee of $15 for every new customer you bring in that hasn't been on the website for at least 12 months. With their wide range of products and conversion rates, their affiliate program offers an easier payout, plus you won't actually have to push the products for a sale. They also offer full tech support, and it's easy to join the program as long as your website meets their requirements.

FitBark

Remember how I mentioned expanding on verticals? Well, if you love fitness and pets, you should definitely look into FitBark as an affiliate. Dogs have become a big part of fitness as owners love to take them out for a walk or run, so it shouldn't surprise anyone that a company has managed to corner this specific niche on the market.

FitBark is a GPS tracker that helps keep tabs on people's dogs and their habits, providing detailed health reports. They can track the dog's sleeping pattern and activity levels, which could assist veterinarians to make better decisions when it comes to that dog's health.

This company uses a pay-per-sale model and, though the commission is low, their average sales are mainly at $100, so you can still earn some money. The company also serves over 140 countries, so they have a huge market, giving you a bigger chance of making a sale.

Cuddle Clones

Cuddle Clones is a brand that celebrates the joy of owning a pet. They recognize the unbreakable bond between owners and their furry friends, though that bond could sometimes be disrupted due to travel, deployment, or even loss. This company creates handmade plush replicas of any pet, capturing all the physical details and personality traits of the customer's beloved animal.

This company works a bit differently than other affiliate programs. Affiliates choose their own coupon codes and, whenever that code is used, the customer gets a discount while the affiliate gets a commission. They also provide their affiliates with a unique link to their website that's tied to the affiliate's account. This helps the affiliate track their earnings, and helps Cuddle Clones keep tabs on customers that buy from these links. On top of all that, affiliates will also get their own pages on the Cuddle Clones website with individual photos and exclusive offers ("Cuddle Clones Affiliate" 2021).

Honest Paws Affiliate

Through the Honest Paws Affiliate, partners can earn a commission based on sales generated through their links. With competitive commission rates, pre-made product-specific banners, email templates, and product shots, and frequent affiliate communications, this is a great company to apply to. Affiliates can earn up to 25% from any valid sales through their affiliate links and offer both Revshare and CPA options with premium payouts.

Petplan

This company dabbles in both the pet and insurance vertical. Petplan offers pet parents the most comprehensive coverage in North America, and has shelters in both the United States and Canada. This pet insurance company is trusted by the Tampa Bay and Jacksonville Humane Society, the Ontario SPCA, and North Shore Animal League.

Those who want to become a partner with PetPlan must apply through their affiliate partner, Pepperjam, before they can start. However, the benefits are pretty great. Affiliates are paid for monthly leads via a direct deposit, have access to their real-time performance tracking, and can use any of the premade marketing materials.

Pets Best

Pets Best is another pet insurance company that would be a perfect fit for those with pet-related finance, health, or lifestyle blogs and websites. If you're interested in educating your viewers about the importance of pet insurance, all you need to do is fill out their application form to apply for their affiliate program. If they decide you're a good fit, you'll be contacted by a representative to complete the signup process. Once you're an affiliate, you'll have access to their recommended marketing materials and content. Plus, you'll be assigned a unique tracking URL for your website. You'll have access to their reports and receive payments each time someone signs up for pet insurance through your link. Pets Best offers up to $35 or higher for every submitted insurance application.

Are You the Right Fit?

With the pet industry making billions each year, the pet vertical is probably one of the most competitive niches. However, if you're willing to put some work into your website and affiliate links, you could make some good money from this vertical. As long as you continue to remain consistent and dish out relevant content to pet owners, you could have some success as a pet affiliate marketer. You could even branch out into other expertise such as pet insurance, or even CBD, which is a growing industry, as long as you stay up-to-date.

How To Promote As A Pet Affiliate

While it might seem easy to get started as a pet affiliate, and since you have a lot of company programs and top brands to choose from, it might not be an easy success right away. You'll really need to have that right frame of mind of a pet owner who really loves and cares for their pets. To really be successful, you'll need to prove to your viewers that you can be trusted to promote the best and safest products for their fur babies, using your own real-life experiences when reviewing pet products, accessories, or food. If you're already a pet owner, empathizing and adding a personal touch to your pet-related web content might come easy. If you're not, you might need to research the topic to be able to offer reliable tips to actual pet owners.

You might also want to research how to use social media sites like Instagram, Pinterest, and Facebook to help promote your affiliate links strategically. Finding some top pet bloggers or pet social media influencers can help give you some insight and inspiration. Ironically, some of the top pet influencers aren't even human, though their accounts might be managed by owners.

Consumers today are getting tired of the cliche and detached advertising nature many companies still try to push. Your viewers will want personalized and engaging content about the products you'll be promoting. You can check out the Oh My Dog blog or The Conscious Cat to begin to understand how personalized content can help market your affiliate products and earn you some money.

There are also several different things you need to consider to be a successful pet affiliate marketer. For one, you'll need to figure out what keywords you should choose to fit your pet affiliate marketing campaign. As I noted above, the pet vertical is highly competitive and you might find it difficult to carve out a space for yourself. So, when it comes to keywords in your blog or website content, you should probably focus on less-competitive ones. If you're just starting out, research the different keywords related to this niche so you don't waste time on your content creation in the beginning.

Another thing you need to think about is what animals you'd like to focus on. Different animal niches are more profitable than others. For example, although the cat niche is profitable, it's still not as big as the dog niche. So, whether you choose to focus on dogs or cats, or any other animal for that matter, it's best to do some pre-planning and research before joining a pet affiliate program.

Once you choose your pet niche, you'll want to focus on your content. Long-form contents like how-to guides and detailed reviews are great for pet affiliate marketers. Content like these usually stay up-to-date and relevant, and are often sought out over and over for extended periods of time, which could definitely help earn you more money. You should also look into using various multimedia content like making videos or having professional images so your blog or website can look more appealing and interesting.

So, if you're a pet owner, or just love animals in general, pet affiliate marketing might just be the perfect thing for you. It's relatively easy to get into, especially when you already have real-life experiences from caring for and loving your own pet to use as personalized content. You can grow a trusted and reliable blog or website, which will then establish a trust between you and the viewers you're hoping will use your affiliate links. Just remember to stay relevant and trustworthy.

4

EBOOKS

MANY PEOPLE DREAM of someday publishing their own book—whether it's a nonfiction how-to book such as this, or an adventurous fiction novel. Publishing used to be rather difficult. Major publishers were gatekeepers. Those who just wanted to write could not get through. Some companies accept. Now, it's easier than ever, and you can publish your book in more than one way.

While I can't help you actually write one, I can give you the basic how-to in publishing your own ebook. Writing an entire book is an accomplishment and one you should definitely be proud of, but it's only the first of many steps in actually getting that manuscript out into the world. You'll need to publish it, converting it from a typed work into a beautifully designed ebook. And, even after you publish it, the work won't be done yet.

This chapter will cover everything from what an ebook actually is, understanding why and how they work, and how to actually publish your own. We'll even take it a step further and explain how you can begin marketing your new book, and what to do after.

So, let's begin with the basics, shall we?

What is an Ebook?

Nowadays, everything is electronic: eCommerce, eBanking, eTickets...we even have eGift Cards. The list is endless. But why? Why have we suddenly entered into this digital age where everything seems to revolve around technology? Well, most people really do love the idea that everything they need is accessible virtually anywhere at the edge of their fingertips.

Even our leisure activities have gone digital, especially reading. Though many people enjoy holding physical books in their hands, those copies aren't always readily available or logical to carry around all the time. Ebooks allow us to carry multiple books in our pocket, easily accessible to anyone with an electronic device.

But what exactly is an ebook?

It might seem pretty straightforward. An ebook is an electronic book. However, the more detailed definition would be a non-editable, reflowable manuscript that's been converted into a digital format and read on any digital device.

Ebooks are basically files you can read on your computer, phone, or even your e-reader—something that's specifically used to read electronic books. But, unlike most files such as Word documents, ebooks aren't editable. If you're publishing something that is uniquely yours, you wouldn't want anyone to simply change your content. So, just like a paperback, ebooks shouldn't be changed in any way (Omukhango 2021).

Another defining characteristic of ebooks is that they should always be reflowable. This means that your text has the ability to automatically wrap words to the next line no matter what size screen your reader is using. Most ebook publishers require manuscript files to be reflowable.

To fit these two characteristics, there are several ebook formats authors can use. However, to keep things simple, we'll just cover the three main ones that are well-known for being easy to use and have the ability to be widely distributed.

First is your EPUB (.epub). EPUB, short for electronic publication, is one of the most widely supported ebook formats that can be read on different types of devices. These files are reflowable, which fits the definition of what an ebook is, and allows the manuscript to be easily read on smaller screens. The next is the AZW (.azw) file. Developed by Amazon for Kindle, these files can store more complex content such as bookmarks, annotations, and highlights— something generally used on Amazon's eReaders. However, the AZW files are strictly limited to Kindles or other devices that use Kindle apps. Plus, these files are only really accepted by Amazon, though it is one of the biggest ebook publishers on the market. Lastly, you could also format your ebook using PDF. Though a PDF wouldn't exactly be considered a true ebook, it's still a format that's widely accepted by ebook publishers. Just remember, these types of files aren't reflowable and will be difficult to read on smaller screens such as cell phones.

Benefits of Ebooks

While holding a physical copy of your ebook will always feel great, there are some benefits in creating an ebook. For starters, you'll be able to reach a wider and more global audience. Those who buy ebooks online will be able to access your book from all over the world, making it more accessible and, in return, making you more money. Many people will actually prefer ebooks as they're less expensive than paperbacks or hardcovers and can actually help save the environment. Plus, you won't need to calculate the costs of paper, ink, and distribution that most self-publishers charge for physical books.

Creating and publishing an ebook can be super beneficial to you if you're hoping to branch out into being an author. As I noted above, ebooks will save you money on publishing. Usually, when you publish a book, you'd need to give a portion of your earnings to the printer and distributor. Ebooks cut out that middle man, giving you most of your pay straight to your own bank account. No need to pay for paper and ink—it's all digital.

On top of all that, ebooks make it easier for people to search for your book and instantly download it. Marketing your book online in this form will help you expand your audience, allowing more people to find your book in online searches and snag it right away. No more waiting for shipping. No more missed sales. Ebooks allow you to use certain keywords where readers can easily find your book.

Why Create an Ebook?

So, we went over the benefits ebooks have over physical copies, but now let's discuss why it's such a great idea to actually write and publish one. Whether it's a simple self-help guide or a creative idea you'd spent years on, self-publishing your ebook is a great idea for anyone who wants to share their vision with the world.

Since ebooks are easily searchable and accessible, new authors can broaden their audiences by simply publishing their manuscripts online. Not only that but writing, in general, is a great way to expand your own knowledge and establish expertise in whatever field you're writing about. Plus, you get to develop your writing and editing skills as well.

Besides all that, ebooks are becoming more popular as part of marketing strategies. They're great assets when it comes to attracting customers or fans for your brand or career. If you do it right, you could turn readers into possible customers or clients. If your content is informative and valuable, you could attract readers to your website or your company, turning them into potential leads, which is a great marketing strategy.

How Much Can You Earn?

There are various platforms on which you can publish your ebook, however, the biggest one is Amazon Direct Publishing (KDP). Kindle Direct Publishing, a branch of Amazon, will pay you up to 70% for each book you manage to sell. Yet, since ebooks are generally priced lower than physical ones, most only make about $2 per sale. Not too bad for something you completed in just a few weeks.

How to Make an Ebook

It can seem a bit overwhelming to learn how to write and publish an ebook. However, they're actually not that hard to put together and market with just a little bit of guidance. The process starts with developing your content. Who will your audience be? What sort of message do you want to send out into the world? Knowing these types of goals for your book can help you in choosing a topic and demographic you'd be marketing towards.

Once you've chosen your topic, you'll need to figure out a title. You'll want something that catches your reader's eyes and will pull them in. It should give them a reason why they'd want to buy and read your book.

After, you'll want to outline your ebook in order to effectively plan your writing schedule. Breaking your ebook into chapters with a step-by-step guide on what you're going to write about will help you complete the book faster than if you were flying from the seat of your pants. Plus, creating this outline will save you the time and hassle of making things up or researching off the top of your head.

Now comes the fun part: actually writing your ebook. This is your chance to show your readers that you're an expert on your subject, or simply entertain them. Whatever you choose to do, be sure to include details, be creative, and really wow them.

When you finally have an edited and completed manuscript, you'll want to start looking into the exterior and interior designs for your book. Ebooks will only require a front cover, saving you time and money in putting more effort into designing the spine and back of the book. You'll want clear and high-resolution images for your cover, something that will be eye-catching but not overwhelming. You'll also want to be sure that the images you use are licensed for commercial use. To make your book easier to read, consider researching how to format ebooks, or you can hire professionals to help you online.

Finally, you'll have your fully converted and finished ebook, cover, and all. Now, all that's left to do is market and promote your book to your target demographic.

Finding Content

This is probably the most difficult step when it comes to creating an ebook. You might be excited to start writing, to really start pounding out that manuscript. But...what should you write about?

That's the beauty of being an author. You can write about almost anything you want to, as long as you have the creativeness and resources to do your research. With self-publishing, there are no literary agents or publishers that will dictate what you can and cannot write about. You have complete creative control.

Any knowledge or idea you have floating around in your head can be turned into an ebook. All you have to do is sit down and map it out into one cohesive manuscript.

Creating a Title

Once you have a rough idea of what you want to write about, the next step would be to come up with a title. Vague or boring titles won't cut it, though. You'll need something that hints about what's inside of your book while simultaneously catching the attention of your reader.

There are a few things you could possibly do when coming up with a title for your ebook. First, you can check out some of the other books in the genre you're planning on publishing in. Checking out what seems to work, or certain trends will be extremely helpful in creating your title. Or, you could try some title generators online.

Creating Your Outline

When you're creating an outline, there are two different ways you could do this. First, you could map everything out, down to every last detail. This can be extremely helpful in the long run, however, you could also start to feel burnout by spending so much time on just the outline. On the other hand, you could vaguely plot out each chapter, keeping the details to the bare minimum, and just getting out the main points. But this could lead to you getting stuck in the middle, or spending too much time doing research you should have done before.

Having a nice mix of both ways would help you. Map out your ebook chapter by chapter by adding in the key points and some minor but important details. This will help save you a lot of time during your actual writing process and it will prevent you from feeling too overwhelmed or bored before you even start writing.

One simple way of creating an outline is to take all your highlights and put them on note cards. And, nowadays, you won't even need to physically write on actual paper cards. You could use an application called Scrivener, among others, that helps with outlining and actually writing your manuscript.

Create a Writing Schedule

Finding the time to actually write a book can be super difficult. But, in order to get the job done, you'll need to develop a writing schedule that won't make you feel overwhelmed or stressed, and that fits your normal daily schedule. You might not feel as if you have time. But that's the thing with writing—no one has time. You have to make time.

If you're worried about burning out, try just taking an hour a day. Or, try setting a word goal such as writing one thousand words a day. And, if you're the type of person who needs a bit more structure, setting a deadline can help you stick to a schedule, encouraging you to actually meet your goals.

Some people find that the easiest time to write is between 10 P.M and 8 A.M. But you don't necessarily have to write between those times. Writing in between shifts, before breakfast, or even on your work breaks can work just as well. You just need a schedule that fits you and eases the stress of actually writing.

Editing

Once you've completed your manuscript (hopefully by your deadline!) the easy and cheapest option is to edit the book yourself. However, I would highly look into hiring a professional editor. For self-published authors, there's a lot of scrutiny about the legitimacy of the books they publish. Having a pristine and professionally edited ebook will not only help you boost sales but make you seem more legitimate to your readers.

If you do want to self-edit your book, check out applications such as Grammarly. Grammarly has a free version that not only checks for spelling and other grammar mistakes but also makes sure your word choices are correct based on the surrounding content. They also include vocabulary enhancement tools. The premium version of Grammarly will also check for punctuation, sentence structure, and style.

Sometimes applications won't catch everything, however. If you're still looking for a cheaper option for editing, try giving your friends and family a copy of your manuscript. They might be able to spot mistakes you might have missed and give you overall feedback on how your book is in general.

Cover Design

Unless you're a super creative person with Adobe superpowers, I would highly suggest hiring a professional book cover artist or graphic designer who has experience and knowledge of book layouts. If you're going to attempt to make a book cover yourself, just remember that—in the book world—people really do judge a book by its cover. Actually, when it comes to readers, every book is judged by its cover.

Nowadays, many book lovers will simply buy a book because they love the cover, without ever having actually read what it's about. Plus, having a professional book cover will help you with that legitimacy issue I mentioned self-published authors really struggle with.

If you're looking for some great book cover designers, there are a few places you can check out. Fiverr or Upwork is always a great idea. You can find smaller businesses that offer cheaper services or professionals charging the big bucks if money isn't an issue. Other places to check out would include 99designs where you can run a contest for designers and choose the best design.

Formatting Your Ebook

Once your book is completely written and edited, you're going to want to convert it into an actual ebook. If you've written your manuscript in Word, you can use Amazon's Kindle Create to format your book, or you can keep it simple and format it in Word. However, Kindle Create is a great tool to use as it lets you preview and edit your books as they will appear on the Kindle apps, create and edit a table of contents, and add professionally designed themes to help make your ebook look more professional.

If you don't want to format your book yourself (it does get a bit difficult at this stage), then you can always hire professionals online who are experts in formatting print and ebooks for self-published authors. You can go back to Fiverr and Upwork to find these professionals, but just be prepared to spend a little bit more money on this service.

Pricing

So, you've finished writing and editing, found a unique and creative cover, and formatted your ebook. Now you just need to figure out the price. Technically, you can price your ebook however much or little you want, but you still want to be making some royalties from it. For Amazon, the sweet spot for pricing is usually between $0.99 and $2.99.

Description

You'll also want to create an engaging and interesting description for your ebook. Once your cover catches a reader's attention, you'll want to keep it before they decide to buy it or not. Take your time writing your description, often called a blurb. This will give your readers an insight into what your book is about and grab their attention. If you're unsure how to write a description, check out Amazon's Top 100 book list for inspiration.

Online Tools for Publishing

If you're wanting to publish your book on other sites besides just Amazon's Direct Publishing, you're in luck. Before, there weren't many places a self-published author could actually publish and distribute their books. Now, there are a few you can choose from.

BookBaby is just one of many sites that provides professional services for self-published authors. Besides simply helping in distributing your book, they can also help you convert your manuscript into the correct formats. Your book will be listed on their online catalog, where other businesses and companies list books on their own personal sites, such as Barnes & Noble.

Smashwords is another ebook distributor that sells to major online bookstores. Rather than paying an upfront fee, you'll pay a percentage of your royalties, sort of like how Amazon's Direct Publishing works. Another great distributor would be Ingram Spark. Though there is a hefty fee to actually publish your book here, they do have a wide reach when it comes to distribution.

As you can see, you're not just limited to publishing on Amazon, though that is still one of the biggest book publishing and buying sites, even today.

Marketing Your Ebook

Although many authors think that, once they're done writing, they can just publish their books and watch the passive income roll right on in. However, that's not really the case. Just as a lot of work goes into writing your book, it's the same for what comes after. The task of marketing might seem overwhelming or daunting, but eventually, it can actually become fun. There are so many different ways to market your ebook.

First, you'll want to create an author website. Your website should include a page about you, the author, and details about your book, or books. Once you have your website, create a powerful sales page. Many authors will link their book's Amazon page to their website. You should include your book's cover, description, and provide some excerpts from good reviews.

Another way to market your book is to reach out to some book bloggers. There are a ton of enthusiastic readers who run blogs, or even entire Instagram accounts solely based around reviewing books. Utilizing social media, like Instagram and Facebook, will help immensely when marketing your ebook. And, luckily, there are a ton of book bloggers and reviewers on both! Some will require a fee in order to review your books, while others will simply ask for a copy of your book for free. When choosing a book blogger, be sure to check out their reach online to see how many potential leads you can create from just one or a few posts from your blogger.

When marketing, you'll want to also build your audience online. You can do this in a number of ways. As I mentioned above, you'll want to fully utilize your social media accounts. Consistent posting of creative content is key here. And, nowadays, many authors are even creating short videos to post on their social media accounts to really draw in readers and create interest. You'll also want to grow your own blog or email list (or both). Creating your own blog to post updates on your book and other writing work will help encourage readers to then subscribe to your blog or email list. This will allow you to easily reach out to your readers who want to support you, and they can ultimately help you with marketing by sharing your book.

Another good resource is Goodreads. Goodreads is a vast online book catalog where many book lovers go to post detailed reviews or to check and see if a book is worth reading. You can ask your book bloggers or reviewers to leave a review on Goodreads after they've read your book. And, you can also run giveaways on Goodreads to help boost and promote your ebook.

5

AUDIOBOOKS

JUST LIKE AN EBOOK, audiobooks are becoming more popular among readers. Actually, out of the three different book formats, it's had the highest growth in the last few years. And, unless you've been living in a cave, you've probably started hearing a lot more about this book format.

Sort of like podcasts, people have started to enjoy listening to books on the go—whether they're in their car on the way to work or simply listening while they work around the house. It's no wonder that the audiobook market has continued to grow at a rate of 30% per year (Hamilton 2021). But what exactly is an audiobook? And why should you make one?

Audiobooks are exactly what it sounds like—books that are voice recorded rather than physical or electron print. Audiobooks could be word-for-word versions of print or ebooks or abridged versions. And, you can listen to an audiobook on almost any electronic device.

Audiobooks are usually purchased and downloaded just like ebooks and music. They can be purchased from online bookstores or down-loaded from websites such as Amazon Kindle. And now, even public libraries are starting to offer audiobook downloads online as long as you have a library card. Even Spotify has an audiobook section.

Audiobooks are available in various different formats such as MP3, Windows Media Audio (WMA), and AAC (Advanced Audio Coding). Most electronic devices are built to recognize any of these options as well.

WAV files go back all the way to 1991, in the early Microsoft days. You might remember, you might not. If you were around during this time, you might remember the various sounds when there was an error. These sounds were WAV files. This type of format worked great for short sounds because WAV is enormous.

Nowadays, WAV files are typically used as the uncompressed file that stores all sorts of recording that is then used by an audio engineer during file mastering (Hamilton 2021). That might sound confusing, especially if you don't exactly know how all of this works in the first place. It would be easier to describe what happens when you actually record.

Let's say you've recorded something in GarageBand. These files are typically '.band' files which are then used by the audio engineer to extract the individual WAV tracks for each book's chapter. Those files are mastered and then exported as MP3 files or M4B files (Hamilton 2021).

MP3 files, as I just stated above, are the final audio format for most audio recordings, including ACX audio. They're much smaller and more compressed than the WAV files, so they're portable and easily downloadable. This was a huge thing back then, and this invention of the MP3 files is what allows us to put thousands of audio onto our smartphones.

M4B files are much like MP3 files in the way that they're much smaller. M4B files, used by iTunes, are what you're usually downloading when purchasing an audiobook from this company's site. With Audible, you're downloading MP3 files. The biggest difference between the two M files is that M4B audio files are able to be bookmarked whereas MP3 cannot. Creating M4B files is pretty difficult to do on your own, though.

However, if you're using the Audiobook Creation Exchange, where most audiobooks are published, to publish your audiobook, they will send your audio files to both iTunes and Audible, so you won't actually have to convert your book yourself. If you do want to create an M4B file on your own for any reason, there are some programs available that will export the WAV files as M4B once they've been mastered.

Although audiobooks have only recently enjoyed a burst of popularity in recent years, did you know that they've actually been around since the 1930s? They were often used in educational settings, found in schools and libraries. Before audiobooks were available digitally, like ebooks, they were often sold in a physical form like cassette tapes or vinyl records. However, nowadays, audiobooks are available in many different ways.

Why Make an Audiobook

Now that we've covered what an audiobook is, you're probably wondering why you should actually make one. The answer is simple: if you're not creating audiobooks, you're missing out on some passive income and ultimately excluding a vast amount of potential readers. With millions of audiobook listeners around the globe, from a business point of view, creating an audiobook just seems a bit obvious.

With the continuation of technology's advancement, there's really no end in sight to the growth of the audiobook. Even though the formats in which we listen to them continue to change, many readers now actually prefer audiobooks compared to any other format. However, not just any book can make a great audiobook.

Some genres, or types of books, will make it difficult to turn into an audiobook. In fact, Audible, an audiobook company, actually recommends not making any of these types of books into an audiobook. Genres such as reference books, quotation books, image-heavy books such as gardening or interior design books and picture books, cookbooks, and travel guides. If your ebook falls into any of these categories, you most likely won't want to make an audiobook for your manuscript.

If your book doesn't fall into any of the above categories, then you might have the recipe for a great audiobook. While there will always be some variances to how well one genre does against others, these genres typically do well, especially on Audible, which we will get more into later.

If your book is a self-help or spiritual guide, history or biography, mystery or thriller, fantasy, science fiction, anything about health and fitness that isn't picture heavy, romance, or even business, then you should be fine. To decide whether or not your audiobook will do well, you need to think about your target demographic.

Will your readers be mostly businessmen and women listening to your business audiobook on the way to work? Will they be mothers or fathers who enjoy listening to a good romance novel while completing chores around the house? Or perhaps you'd simply like to be more inclusive to readers who are disabled and need the assistance of audiobooks. Whoever your target demographic is, that's what should help you decide on making an audiobook or not.

Tools of the Trade

Like ebooks, when it comes to making audiobooks there are literally hundreds of different software and hardware that you can use to produce and create. I'll go over some tools you'll be able to use, especially if you own a MAC computer. If you're using a computer that has Windows, you'll still be able to substitute any of these for a Windows platform easily. The important points of creating an audiobook apply to virtually any combination of different software and hardware.

The generic tools you'll need to professionally record your audiobook include a computer with a USB port, and a high-quality microphone with a stand and a pop filter—the little round cloth in front of the mic) (Bennett 2021). You'll also need to record in an environment that will have little to no background noise and won't have an echo. You will also need recording software, editing software, and audiobook creation software.

If you're interested in making an audiobook, you could always take the easier route and hire a voice artist to record it for you. Though this isn't the cheapest way, it can ease the stress of actually making one yourself. You'll need to find a good narrator who knows what they're doing. They then record the book. The files will then be converted by an audiobook engineer. When they're finished, you'll then have a completed audiobook file, including the rights.

The majority of audiobooks are published on the Audiobook Creation Exchange (ACX) (Hamilton 2021). That's also where you can find narrators for your own audiobook. There are also several other companies that specialize in audiobook production. The advantage to hiring a private company is that they will usually do any book at any sort of length, even if it's super short. Plus, they're more likely to offer contracts. However, they will typically employ fewer narrators than the thousands you can choose from on ACX. And, ACX offers more options for audiobook narration. However, many of these narrators aren't interested in working on shorter books and many will request a share of your royalties.

Generally, a high-quality audiobook could be recorded at the rate of $300 per 10,000 words (Hamilton 2021). This is usually a good benchmark to go by, though there might be some narrators and companies that will charge more or less. It all depends and it would be wise to do your own research if you're planning on outsourcing your audiobook.

Yet, if you're a do-it-yourselfer and want to try out the illustrious career of voice narration for yourself, here are some things you need to know before you begin. Since Audible is one of the primary distributors of audiobooks, and because their requirements will assist you in creating more professional and high-quality audiobooks, I'll be going over those. Below are both the audio and image requirements needed. These requirements only include what's needed to create the files, not how to submit them to Audible, which we will cover later.

First and foremost, all recordings must have a human voice. You cannot use computer-read books when submitting to Audible and other audiobook publishing sites. The file that is typically accepted is an MP3 of 193 kbps or higher, and your files must be a constant bit rate (CBR). Your submitted audiobook must not contain both mono and stereo files together. These types of files must not be joint, either. Mono files are preferred and often required. Each file must include a single section such as a chapter or episode of the book. Each file will generally come with a track that a customer can use for navigation. If your book doesn't really have chapters, you'll need to split the audio into segments that are two hours or shorter. However, these segments cannot be shorter than thirty minutes if possible.

Next, your files should be preceded by a three-digit number that will tell the listener in what order the files should appear (Bennett 2021). Your audio should be free of sounds such as mouse clicks, mic pops, or mouth noises. For the noise floor, the measure should be between -23dB and -18dB RMS and have a -3dB peak value with a maximum of -60db. And, lastly, each file should have between .0.5 and 1 second of room tone at the start of the recording, and between 1 to 5 seconds in the end.

Besides audio requirements, there are also a few image requirements needed when publishing your audiobook. The images cannot be smaller than 2400 X 24000 pixels. They must have a resolution smaller than 72 dpi and they must be squared. These covers cannot be rectangular with colored borders on the sides like a CD case cover (Bennett 2021). Your images should also be at least 24-bit and only three image formats are allowed: JPEG, TIFF, and PNG. Finally, your image must include both your book title and your author name.

Narrating and Recording Your Audiobook

As an author, it might be tempting to record your own book. You'll know exactly how you want it to read, or what tone of voice you want to use and where. You need to realize, however, that narrating an audiobook is not the same as speaking or singing. Reading, whether it be fiction or nonfiction, has some sort of acting element to it. And your readers won't enjoy your audiobook if there's a bad actor behind the voice. However, if you believe you can sound authentic, and if other people agree, then go right ahead—read away! If not, I would highly suggest outsourcing this part to a professional with experience.

When adapting your book for audio, there might be one or more things that will need to be changed. Some of these include references to pages. Rather than saying "see page 5 for more details", it would have to be changed to something like "this will be further discussed in chapter 8" (Bennett 2021). Another thing that will have to be changed is any charts or graphs. You might possibly consider leaving these out, or you could simply describe these to your listeners. Or, you could include these as a PDF that comes with the audiobook, though few people actually open these.

With audiobooks, you won't really need a table of contents or glossary. And, you'll also want to leave out super long lists that aren't really meant to be read and are there just for a certain effect. For example, listing all those who fought in World War II, or other such things. However, it would be up to you to decide how you want to handle these based on how you want your audiobook to be read.

If you decide to narrate your own audiobook, there are some other complications you could run into. For one, many people might experience changes in their voices after reading over a prolonged amount of time. Sometimes, these changes aren't so subtle. You don't want your completed audiobook to sound as if there were multiple narrators. This means you'll need to record in the same conditions each day and avoid straining your voice.

Another complication could be making mistakes when narrating. Most of these you'll notice right away, such as stumbling over words or stressing the wrong syllable. When you make mistakes, it would be easy enough to just edit it in real-time or repeat the sentence and keep going. I would suggest repeating the sentence before moving one as editing in real-time can mess with whatever flow you've gotten into and could leave your finished audiobook sounding too choppy. When you do make a mistake, it's very important to pause before repeating the sentence. Otherwise, when you're trying to edit it later, it could be a nightmare and you might have to rerecord many other sections.

If you're a newbie at recording audio, I would highly suggest using GarageBand by Apple. It's simple and cheap, but powerful. However, the newer version has removed a lot of the podcast and voice recording features that the '09 version has. You could also use a software called Audacity to record and edit as well, which doesn't require you to have any Apple products.

If you're working with a small book, one that might be less than 4 hours of recording time, it might make sense to use one source file for the entire book. So you'd make one file with the title of your book and that would be it. However, if you're planning on converting a bigger book into an audiobook, one source file might not be enough. These recording software will often have limits to how large and long a file can be. Plus, working with large files can be really difficult to edit later on. This means that your audiobook might require multiple files, which might work best by splitting them into chapters or sections.

After you've recorded your audiobook, you'd then have to edit it. In the editing process, you'll create the final sound files that you'll need to combine into one folder. For most audiobook publishing sites, you'll need individual source files for your opening credits, chapters or sections, foreword, dedication, or any other parts of your book.

The best way to review your recording is by reading along as you go through it. Sometimes, you might find that you've skipped a word, though it might still sound alright. By reading along, you can ensure that you've covered everything you want to and will help you pick up any more errors you might have missed.

But you don't want to just listen to find possible mistakes. You'll also want to review the smoothness of the edits, pronunciations of your words, and inflection. At this point, you'll need to accept that there might be more editing in your future, sometimes involving several parts of the book. When you come across something you feel needs to be redone, make a note to change it later on.

Once your audiobook is complete, you can then export it. Don't worry about the silence at the beginning and end of your recording, you can do that later on. Just be sure that your export settings meet the technical requirements I've listed above, and be sure to export your files into a single folder. It's also a good idea to constantly be saving your edited source files so you won't lose any progress if the software or your computer crashes.

After editing, you'll need to add that silence to the start and end of your book, as Audible requires. Whether you plan to publish your audiobook through Audible or not, it's a good rule to follow in general. You'll want to aim for .75 seconds of space at the beginning and 3 seconds at the end (Bennett 2021).

Next, you need to normalize your audio. You probably thought you were done, right? Not quite. With Audible, each file must measure between -23dB and -18dB RMS with -3dB peak values and a maximum of -60dB noise floor (Bennett 2021). Once again, even if you're not going through Audible, this is a good requirement to have. Usually, you will go to Effect>Normalize in the software you're using and simply set the normalize value to -3. Then click OK and you'll be done.

Putting Together Your Audiobook

Once you have all these recordings done, you'll be left with a plethora of files—but not an actual audiobook. Though many people who listen to audiobooks on their computers would be fine with having a bunch of MP3 files, you'll want to be sure that you're following the requirements for whatever audiobook publishing you'll be using. Some will allow MP3 files, while others will help you to convert these formats into M4B.

If you want to try and convert these MP3 files on your own, you could use the app Audiobook Builder, which is available in the Apple App Store. You will fill in the title of your book, as well as the genre and your author name. You will also upload the cover. Once you upload all your source files and click OK, you'll then have a complete audiobook.

Audiobook Markets

Though there are many audiobook markets out there, like ebooks, Amazon is the giant in the book publishing world. Audible, one of the popular audiobook sites is also owned by Amazon, with ACX, yet another audiobook publishing company, being owned by Audible. ACX is the audiobook version of Kindle Direct Publishing. ACX holds your audiobook files, cover, and data. However, ACX also distributes to iTunes, which is just one example of the Apple-Amazon collaboration, making it difficult for other audiobook companies to compete.

There are some other companies worth mentioning, though none are as big as ACX or Audible. The other biggest players include Overdrive, Audiobooks.com, Downpour, and Chirp. You might have also heard about Findaway Voices.

Overdrive is the main application that distributes to libraries, which could be a great opportunity to get your audiobook more widely distributed. However, Overdrive is extremely selective when it comes to choosing what authors they accept. Typically, you're going to need at least a dozen or more audiobooks already recorded in order to attempt to get your audiobooks on Overdrive.

Audiobooks.com comes in second place behind ACX when it comes to audiobook sales, though ACX is way ahead in this game. This audiobook service was one of the first-ever platforms that initiated the idea of giving readers a faster and easier way of accessing audiobooks. Readers can download thousands of different audiobooks at a super low price—which might not be that great when it comes time to earn royalties, but could still be a good option.

Downpour is another platform that's right behind Audiobooks.com in sales, though you might have to negotiate a deal to be published by them (Hamilton 2021). On ACX you can just publish your audiobook and start selling immediately, though some sites will require a contract such as Audiobooks.com.

Chirp, however, will be a bit different. They take your finished audiobook and see if it's eligible for any deals. While they're a sales platform with their own audiobook app, they're run by the same company behind BookBub, an ebook and print publishing company. So it's generally geared more towards deal seekers. However, their reach is fairly large and, if you manage to get featured, it could be super lucrative for you in the long run (Hamilton 2021). But, in order to be on Chirp, you'll need to first be on Findaway Voices.

Unlike the other sites I've mentioned, Findaway Voices is not a sales platform. Instead, it's a production and distribution channel. They help you create your audiobook recording by giving you a wide selection of professional narrators. Or, if you've already completed an audiobook with another narrator, it will still distribute your audiobook to other sites.

Besides ACX, there aren't that many audiobook publishers that become huge sellers for authors. However, using all of them together can still make you some money. But setting up or sending your files to all these different vendors could be such a hassle. Findaway Voices saves you the time and effort in uploading your files to all these different sites. If you're not wanting to be exclusive with ACX, this is a great option for you to consider.

How Much Can You Make?

So, now on to the big question: how much can you actually make with audiobooks? With ACX, they will choose the price for you based on the runtime of your audiobook (Hamilton 2021). For example, if your book is under one hour, your book will be priced between $3.95 to $7. If it's between one to three hours, it will be priced between $7 to $10, and so on.

Your royalties will then be based on the different ways your book is downloaded or bought. This means that, on Audible at least, your royalties are based on whether a listener is an Audible subscriber, and which location they bought your book from. Audible does offer you a $75 bonus when a listener signs up for an Audible membership and purchases your book as their first buy. This could potentially add up over time.

Audiobook Marketing

Like with an ebook, once you've published your audiobook, you'll need to begin marketing it. If you go through ACX, you'll receive an email from them in about seven to ten days with twenty-five promotional codes you can distribute to potential listeners. This would be a great opportunity to maximize your marketing strategy. You can use these codes to build up your email list, gather reviews for your audiobook, or reward your loyal readers and listeners.

However, unlike with books, marketing for audiobooks is still somewhat new. Unlike KDP, ACX doesn't have a built-in promotional method like Kindle offers. So, basically, you're going to have to put in more time and effort into promoting your audiobook than you might have to with your ebook. There are, however, a few websites you can use to gather some reviews, which you can then utilize for a marketing strategy.

Free Audiobook Promotion Websites

Goodreads has a great audiobook section where you can gather and receive solid reviews. Many people with a love for audiobooks, called audiophiles, tend to gather there, much like how book lovers use Goodreads the most to review their favorite physical or ebooks. Another great review site you might not have even considered is Reddit. Reddit has an audiobooks thread where you can post your book. However, Reddit can also get pretty nasty, so be sure that your book is professional and well-done before posting.

Another thing you can do is create a Facebook group to do Audiobook giveaways. There are even some already-made Facebook groups where you can start promoting your audiobook. Other great social media sites to start getting into include Instagram and TikTok. With Instagram's reel feature, and with TikTok being a video-based platform, you can create interesting videos using parts of your audiobook as sounds, which could then get more people interested in actually purchasing your audiobook.

Though marketing for audiobooks is a concept that's still in the beginning stages, there's so much you can do. Plus, if you're marketing your ebook, or a physical book, alongside it, you can reach a broader market and widen your target demographic. There's really no end to which you can market your books.

6

STARTING YOUR OWN PODCAST

IF YOU'VE GOT ideas or topics but don't really see yourself as a writer, there's another way to get your ideas out into the world: podcasting. Podcasts are episodes of something that's similar to a radio station, but available online. They're usually audio or video recordings with each episode being offered in the same file format, either audio or video so that subscribers can enjoy the program, in the same way, each time. However, some podcasts—like language courses—include multiple different formats.

But what exactly are podcasts? Podcasts are blogs, shows, or topics wrapped up in nice recordings that are released sort of like television shows. You can explore, download, and listen to episodes while on the go on any sort of electronic device. Think of it as audiobook chapters that can be listened to or watched for free by listeners or viewers.

But wait, did I say free? So, how does this make you any money? Like many of the ideas in this book, podcasting is not a way to make money fast. Making money in this field takes time, and you'll need to build loyal and engaged followers—sort of like building an author platform for an ebook or audiobook. And, even then, earning a living through podcasting can be a long and rocky road.

Most podcasters earn their money through advertisements or sponsorships—those affiliate links we discussed in previous chapters. It's possible to make some extra money while podcasting by using these affiliate links. You could even partner with Amazon Associates as they sponsor podcasts that have as little as 1,000 downloads per episode. That might not seem like a lot, but in reality, only about 20% of podcasts actually hit that mark.

As I mentioned previously, affiliate marketing is where you get paid for referring your listeners to another company's product or services. You can find some affiliates through the companies mentioned in previous chapters, or through Buzzsprout or Podcorn. Affiliate links for podcasting will work differently from when you use them for your blog or website.

For podcasts, you'll host a show and mention your affiliate's product. You tell your listeners where they can buy the linked services using your personal code or link. If one of your listeners uses that link, you earn a small commission—like how it works with the blog or website. However, the content you'll be creating will obviously be very different, and you'll need a place to put your affiliate link as you most likely won't be using a website to host your podcasts.

Similar to affiliate marketing, you could try to gain sponsors to pay you to mention their products or services during your shows (Sheehy 2021). Sponsors will generally pay $18 to $25 for every thousand downloads per month (CPM). The more downloads your episodes get, the more money you can make. Unlike affiliate marketing, however, sponsors will essentially pay for potential business rather than just a click on your link. This leads to a risk that your listeners might not be likely to buy anything, which is why advertisers are pickier with what shows they invest in.

Another way you can make income from your podcast is by creating merchandise that is specific to your brand. Having a logo, and an audience that's loyal enough to wear it will help you earn some extra cash while not really having to do much at all. You can create anything from mugs to hats, clothing to pillows. But this means you'll also need an e-commerce store on top of hosting your podcast.

There are various different sites you can use to sell your designs and merchandise. Some places will print and distribute these designs for you, such as Printify, Shopify, or Spring. Some of these will even host your store, and help you design the products using templates.

These are just a few ways you can monetize your podcast. The more creative and interesting content you make, and the more loyal listeners you build up, can help increase that passive income. It all depends on your ideas and what you do with them.

If you've always been interested in, or have just started to become more interested in, starting a podcast, you might be itching to just jump in. However, you can't simply dive into podcasting without noting a few important aspects. Even if your show will only start out as a fun hobby, odds are that you'll eventually want to grow your podcast, making it more successful. A little planning ahead could make a huge difference between a struggling show, and one that has a huge reach, bringing in those sponsorships and cash.

Know Your Audience, Find Your Niche

First, you'll want to ask yourself this question: what is your podcast going to be about? That might seem like the most obvious way to start, however, it's not that easy. You'll want to be specific about the topic of your show, and will want to find a well-defined niche.

It should go without saying, but you might want to simply choose a topic, or topics, that you already have some knowledge or interest in. Then, ask yourself what unique information your podcast will offer to its listeners. Does this topic have enough content to continue making episodes one? Or will it peter out within the first few? Some topics might seem super interesting, and you might know a lot about them, but they won't be able to be stretched out over time.

Finally, you'll want to try and narrow down your topic as much as possible. There are thousands of podcasts on parenting, millions on traveling, and many, many more dedicated to all sorts of themes and genres. It's important for you to find your own niche. For example, if your interests lie in gaming, you might choose a specific genre or style of gaming.

After you've decided on a topic and niche, it's time to think about your target demographic. Who will you be speaking to? Why? Just like how one would want to determine their ideal reader for ebooks or audiobooks, you'll need to figure out who your ideal listener will be. What would they want to hear about? What time of day or night are they most likely to tune it? Think about what their similar interests might be, their age, their location. The more specific you are, the better. The answers to your questions here could help you create some material for the first few episodes.

Create Episode Subjects

Now that you've found a niche, it's time to actually think up some ideas for some episodes. You want to make sure that there's enough material of a topic that you'll be able to discuss for the length of one recording.

To help with brainstorming, think about all the different aspects of the topic you've chosen. If your main focus is something like traveling, try to consider all the things listeners who love to travel might want to know or listen about. A great way to come up with some ideas is to look at blogs or books on the same topic. Now, you don't want to just copy from someone else—that won't be a good way to get real listeners. However, you can draw upon the inspiration chapter or blog titles you can use for your own episodes.

While you're thinking up episode subjects, you'll want to also note how long you want your episode to be as well. Podcast lengths depend solely on your content. Some listeners can only listen to a specific topic for so long, maybe around fifteen minutes, while others can hear about another subject matter for an hour. While there isn't a set limit to how long or short your episodes can be, think about this; many people will listen to podcasts on their commute to work, which is around twenty minutes. So, that might seem to be a good length to shoot for. However, if you have fifty minutes of some interesting content, then you shouldn't try to chop that down—keep the interesting parts! If it's too long, you might be able to split it into two episodes, instead of just one.

Over time, once you build up more listeners, you can make a poll to see what your followers would prefer—longer or shorter episodes. It would be good to find out the average time of what your listeners would like, just so they can know what to expect.

Lastly, while you're thinking of episode ideas, you'll want to think of something that will make your podcast unique, or stand out. The length can actually be a part of this unique factor. Short and snappy five-minute episodes might fit your specific target demographic of twenty-seven-year-old business women or men, who happen to enjoy anything related to cryptocurrency or bitcoin. Or, one-hour episodes might fit your target demographic of elderly grandparents who enjoy listening to anything about plants and botany, with an emphasis on caring for and growing endangered plants. Now, these are just some examples, but you can get the gist.

One question you might be wondering about is when, exactly, you should release new episodes. The best sort of publishing schedule would be one where you're able to consistently post on a regular basis. If you can only manage one episode a month, then post once a month. If you can manage every two weeks or even weekly, then that would be great. The key here is consistency—posting around the same time each month, at the same rate.

While it might be better to try and post weekly, don't keep to this sort of schedule just for the sake of it. You want high-quality podcast episodes, not just a lot of them. It would be better to post one excellent episode for each mother than an average episode every few days. If you're not really one to keep to a specific schedule, however, you could always try seasonal podcasting.

Seasonal podcasting is just what it sounds like—your podcast will only be published during specific times of the year. Much like in the way that some television channels come out with seasonal tv shows or movies for Christmas or Halloween, you'd also post episodes with a seasonal theme, publishing a few episodes, and then wait for the next season you want to do. You can do more than one season. For example, your travel podcast could have a 'where to travel this summer' theme, and then you would wait a few months to discuss autumn festivals around the world that people could travel to and see.

Yet seasonal podcasts aren't just about actual seasons. They can also be about different topics in your general niche. Think of seasonal podcasting like an extended tv series, with your podcast topics traveling in a certain direction.

Pick Your Format & Style

Now that you've thought up some ideas, it's time to figure out how you'll be executing your podcasts. There are several formats and styles your podcast could have. Your format might be educational, storytelling, conversational, or like an interview. You can either host your podcast on your own, or have multiple hosts ("Thinking Of Starting A Podcast? Here Are 7 Things To Know - RSS.Com Podcasting" 2021).

Nowadays, one of the biggest trends in the world of podcasting is that people are co-hosting shows with one or more good friends. The great thing about starting a podcast with friends is that you can split the costs and add more diversity to your podcast episodes. Having different personalities and backgrounds to host your show will add to your unique factor and bring in a bigger audience. Your audience might even develop a preference for their favorite host.

Starting a podcast with your friend, or friends is a great way to earn some extra cash while spending time together. But, there are a few things you should consider. Who will be your hosts? What happens if one person loses interest or wants out? You'll also need to include a financial plan that will cover everything from how you'll divide the costs to how you'll split the profits. Also, consider some common future complications and think of some solutions beforehand. Like, for example, what will happen if one person moves? You'll probably need to invest in software that will allow you to record in separate locations.

If you don't have anyone in mind to help you host your show, going at it alone can be just as successful. Your show could simply just be you sitting at the mic and telling stories, or maybe teaching your audience something you know a lot about. However, be ready to do all of the work that podcasting needs on your own as well. Unless you have a sponsor supporting your podcast from the beginning, you'll most likely have to do all the work alone. This type of podcasting format would be great for those who just want to try it out before diving right in. Then again, some fiction and nonfiction storytellers can produce dozens of episodes on their own and grow a rabid fanbase.

Another type of style you might consider is one that works as an interview. If you'd like to do this, make an interview wish list. Think of the types of people who might have things to add about the topic you've chosen and start making a list. And don't just think small— who knows? Maybe you'll get a big name for your podcast that will help launch you into success. The bigger guest you have, the more potential audience you might get to promote to.

There are some great places when looking for guests. You could check out other podcasts, blogs, YouTube, or Help a Reporter Out. You could also try to collaborate with other podcast hosts, bloggers, or vloggers as well, pooling your viewers together to potentially help each other out. Also, while you're networking, you could try to ask around to see if anyone will have you on their show as well. This will help you network and will give you another way to promote your own podcast.

If you are planning to have a guest speaker on your show you'll need to have a release form. This will help protect you and your show. In the beginning, you can probably just use online templates but, as your show grows, you might want to consult with an attorney who can help create a more specific form for you to use.

You'll also need to schedule these interviews well in advance before your launch. People can be busy, and you don't want to fall behind on your schedule if you can't find someone available. You can even batch several interviews around the same time so you'll have plenty of content if someone has to back out altogether or reschedule.

Having guests on the show can be a great way to market your podcast, so try to have your guests promote these episodes. It will help you to grow your audience faster, and most guests will be more than willing to do that for you. Once the show goes live, try to give them some marketing tools that are already made so they can just simply post about it on their own social media pages or platforms.

Get the Right Equipment

Once you've thought of everything from your topic to your audience and even your content, it's time to start creating. You'll need the right equipment at this stage, which is exactly what we'll go over. To have a good podcast, you'll need quality sound equipment where your listeners won't have to hear too much background noise. You want to be sure that your listeners can hear you clearly without any sort of distractions that might make them turn your episode off.

You'll also want to get a computer with the capability of handling large audio files and editing software, as well as a pop filter (like what I mentioned in the chapter on audiobooks), and a boom or microphone stand. Don't forget that you'll need to purchase a podcast hosting as well, much like what you'd need to begin blogging. RSS Podcasting is one such hosting site. All you'd need to do is upload your audio files via your web browser. These will then show up on your feed automatically. Even if you're planning to post your episodes on iTunes, Google Podcasts, Spotify, or other outlets, you'd still need a host for your show.

When it comes to recording software, there are both free and paid choices you could go with. If you're a MAC user, you could use GarageBand, though as I said before, you'll need the '09 version as newer updates have gotten rid of a lot of their podcasting and voice recording functions. You could also use iMovie or, if you don't own an Apple product, you could use Audacity to help with recording. Alitu is also a great option for more serious podcasters. It does most of the work for you. Or, if you're a pro already, you might want to check out Adobe's subscription plan for Adobe Audition.

While we're talking about recording, now might be a great time to mention that you'll need to think of a good intro and outro to your show. You'll want something that is short but memorable, something that will be uniquely yours. A typical intro will include fun or catchy music as well as your name and the name of your podcast. Some hosts choose to use the same intro over and over for every episode, while others might change them up every season or use new intros for each new show.

The outros are the show's wrap-up and indicate to the listener that the episode is ending. You can add anything you'd like here, including your own website, social media profiles, or anything else you believe would be important to your listeners. This might also be a good time to talk about some affiliated products or sponsors, as well.

If you're going to use music, you'll need to use something called royalty-free, the music you can use for personal use. Some great places to find royalty-free music are Mubert, Bensound, Pixabay, Incompetech, Musopen, Free Music Archive, and CC Mixter. It's important to know that whatever music you're using is not copyrighted, or that you have the right to use this music in your show to avoid lawsuits, fines, or even having your entire podcast shut down.

Turning Your Recordings into Podcasts

Just like with audiobooks, after you finish recording, the next step is —you guessed it—editing. If you don't know much about editing, you could always outsource this to someone who does. It might cost a bit of money, but it will alleviate some of the stress of producing a whole show on your own. You can find some good podcast editors on the Podcast Production Directory, or you can check out Alitu, as I've mentioned before, where they will edit your podcast for you. Alitu is really easy for beginners, and you can record your episodes directly into it. It will process, edit, and publish your shows. It's also got a music library where you can find some tunes for your intro and outro.

After editing, you'll need to find a good place to actually publish your podcast, especially if you aren't going the Alitu route. There are a number of podcast directories you can submit your show to, with millions of potential listeners and fans. I highly recommend adding your episodes to Apple Podcasts first. All you'll need, however, is an Apple ID to submit. If you're using RSS Podcast, you can submit to Apple Podcasts through them as well. Other places include Google Podcasts, Spotify, Stitcher, TuneIn, and Deezer.

For Google Podcasts, once you log in with your Google account, you can visit your dashboard. Click to add your podcast and follow the prompts. The wait for your submission to be reviewed can be anywhere from a day to a week. For Spotify, it can take up to five days to be approved. To be accepted by Spotify, you'll need to have at least one or two episodes ready to publish. If it can't find any episodes, it will reject your submission.

Besides finding a good place to actually publish your podcast, you'll also want to make or find someone to create some good graphics for your show. Most of these sites will require cover art, and you will want some social media images to help market your episodes for Facebook, Twitter, Instagram, or others you want to promote on. You'll also need to include a description of your show as well to tell new listeners what your episodes are all about.

Once you start, the only way is up. Keep researching and producing episodes to grow your own audience. Record and load more episodes, create a marketing strategy to promote them, schedule interviews, and consistently work on your show. And, the more your audience grows, the more money you can make by collaborating with affiliate businesses and gaining sponsors.

7

YOUTUBE

THE PANDEMIC HAS REDIRECTED a lot of people's lives, especially when it comes to how they spend their free time. Before, people might have been too busy to focus on social media, and now they've been forced to spend more time, not just at home, but online as well. One area that has really boomed since the start of the pandemic is YouTube.

Maybe you've already spent a lot of time on the vlogging site, or subscribed to some of your favorite YouTube channels. Maybe you've even had the distant dream of starting your own channel or building your own loyal YouTube following. But there's more than just notoriety that you can gain from growing a YouTube channel—you could make some money from it as well.

Contrary to what you might think, it's not too late to become a YouTube influencer or even build a viable business from YouTube followers, but it's definitely becoming more competitive. In this chapter, we'll go over how to create your own YouTube channel, the different ways you can make some income from your videos, and how to grow your channel.

Why Start a Youtube Channel?

Despite how long YouTube has been around, it's still one of the most popular websites on the Internet. It's got a huge global audience and an app that's installed on pretty much everyone's smartphone. It's even on smart television sets. While it was primarily used to share funny videos in the mid-2000s, it has developed to be almost as influential as TV networks (Freeman-Powell 2021).

Probably the biggest reason to start a YouTube channel, especially if you're wanting to use it to grow your personal business or craft, is that your target audience is already on YouTube. We live in a very audio-visual world, and videos are a key to our online experiences. With internet speeds improving, it's changed the way people spend their time online.

Like, for example, did you know that YouTube is actually the world's second-largest search engine? Of course, Google still holds the first place title, but YouTube has over 2 billion regular monthly users. Over 500 hours of new video content is uploaded to the site every minute (Freeman-Powell 2021). The first thing people use to research is, of course, Google. Google includes different sources to match the search being done—including YouTube videos. With the right metadata, your YouTube videos could pop up in someone's normal Google search, making it easier for new followers to find and subscribe to your channel.

You can further improve your YouTube channel's exposure by linking them to blog posts on your personal or business website. When your viewers click on your links, this increases the authority of your website in Google's eyes, which means that you can increase other pages on your website as well and gain more discovery in general.

As I said, we live in a very visual world. More people prefer to watch short and entertaining videos rather than reading a long, dull page explaining something. Using videos can help make your business seem more interesting. They can reach more people who would otherwise skip over your blogs. This is one way your audience can get to know you better.

Starting a channel is just one way you can form personal and lasting relationships with your audience. It allows you to create longer stories that aren't possible to do with shorter videos such as ads. This is also a great way to make your channel more personal to your viewers, which then could turn them into loyal followers online.

Starting Your Channel

If you've been thinking about diving into the world of YouTube, here's my advice: don't just think—do it. Starting a YouTube channel might seem scary or daunting, but it doesn't have to be. In fact, starting a YouTube channel sort of follows the same starting template as a podcast or writing an ebook.

We'll go over how YouTube actually works, how to find your niche and develop your channel, what equipment you can use, and how to analyze the data of your followers in order to grow your channel. Starting a YouTube channel doesn't have to be too complicated or confusing. It shouldn't stop you from starting what could be a fun and lucrative hobby.

First, you should think about what niche or category you want your channel to be about, just like you would with a podcast or ebook. What will you talk about? What products will you introduce to your followers? From there, you can branch out and cover other categories related to your specific niche to create more content and gain a broader audience. After you decide what your channel will cover, you'll need to actually make your videos.

Most people prefer videos for around ten to fifteen minutes. Any longer and they might get bored, skipping around your video to find the information they want to see or know. Any shorter and it might not capture their attention long enough for them to want to subscribe. So, a mid-length video would be best. Once you finish your video, you can choose to edit it yourself on some software such as Adobe Premiere Pro. This is a subscription service. You can also use YouTubes editor. It comes with tools for blurring out faces, adding end cards, and choosing royalty-free music.

To use YouTube's built-in editor, you'll need to sign in to your YouTube studio page. Click on Content in the left navigation menu and find the video you'd like to edit. On the pop-up menu that appears, you'll be able to click the pencil icon to access the video's details and click Editor in the navigation menu.

YouTube's video editor has some user-friendly controls that will allow you to easily edit your videos on the site. With the video time-line tool, you can scrub through the entire video that comes with a marker for clicking and dragging video footage across the timeline. It also has video speed controls for speeding up or slowing down the video and comes with keyboard shortcuts for faster editing.

While the YouTube editor includes royalty-free music, you cannot add external audio or footage to the YouTube editor. If you want to add last-minute voice-overs or other sound effects, you'll have to add these using a separate software such as Final Cut Pro or Adobe Premiere Pro.

Starting Out

Like most things, your first attempt at creating videos might suck. But hey, at least you made a video! While the art of making a video might take some time to develop over time, you can start by learning the basics of YouTube and creating or growing your YouTube channel. You'll want to develop a strategy that you'll actually follow.

What do you want your channel to show or tell? Try answering this question from your viewer's perspective. Who is your target audience? When thinking about your niche or topics, you'll want to consider what age, gender, and other demographics your viewers might identify with. You'll also want to think about what your potential audience is interested in—who is going to be watching your videos and what do they like?

Another thing to consider is why people should watch your content. Think about it. There are millions and millions of YouTube influencers. How are you going to make your content identifiable and unique? Like with a podcast, you'll need to think about what specialty you're bringing to the table here. What makes your channel unique?

And, finally, how are you going to publish your videos? Again, like with podcasts, you'll need to think about consistency. You should plan out when, exactly, you'll be posting--daily, weekly, monthly. To figure out the best times to post, think about when your viewers will most likely be active.

Once you've answered all these questions above, you'll want to wrap everything up with a nice little bow called a value proposition. You should explain what your channel is about and why people should actually watch your videos. For example, if your niche is about writing books, or reading, you could say your value proposition is "bringing creative new stories to readers" or "reviewing YA books for bibliophiles". Tell your readers who you are.

Investing in the Right Equipment

When starting to create your videos, you might be wondering what type of equipment you'll need. I strongly believe that the real investment you should make is in your sound equipment. Having bad audio in a video can be distracting for viewers, and everybody hates onboard microphones. So, if you can get yourself a decent external microphone for your camera or computer, then you can at least start sounding more professional in your videos.

Another item to invest in is a good camera. You'll want something that was created with the video content in mind and comes with capable image sensors, fast processors, better autofocus, great audio capabilities, a flip-screen, and the ability to shoot in 4K video. You can easily find cameras with all of these features that are still beginner-friendly and affordable to suit your needs as an entry-level vlogger.

Some of the best places to check out camera equipment are Amazon and B&H Photo. B&H Photo is actually a great place to check out high-quality cameras and lenses. They're a reputable company with businesses all over the world and have been around for over forty-five years. Amazon is another great place to look for most of your camera accessories such as filters, memory cards, and tripods.

There are a ton of different cameras you can use to vlog with, but here are some of the more affordable to get you started. The first camera I highly recommend is the Sony ZV-E10. It's a mirrorless camera, which means it has fewer breakable pieces to worry about. It also has 4K video at 30fps, a 3.0" flip-out touch screen, and has an unlimited recording limit. You can find these cameras for around $700 to $800 USD on both Amazon and B&H Photo. On Amazon, these cameras will often come in bundles with a microphone, plus this camera has a live stream function through the USB cable.

Other cameras such as the Canon M50 Mark II and Panasonic Lumix DC-G100 are also good, though they do cap their recording limit at around 10-29 minutes. Still, both of these cameras are also mirror-less with a flip screen and come with Bluetooth and wifi. These are all great beginner cameras for under $1000 USD and can help you create more professional-looking videos.

While you can record videos on your iPhone, I don't really recommend it. First, iPhones record video using .MOV formats, which aren't exactly recognized by editing software such as Adobe Premiere Pro. This can cause problems for you when editing later on. Plus, getting your videos from your camera to your computer might prove to be rather stressful as well. It would be better to invest in the right equipment to make video editing and processing less of a hassle.

Filming

Want to know the secret to YouTube? I can tell you it's not a viral video like many people believe. Instead, the path to making your YouTube channel a success requires effort and creating content that will interest your viewers. Here are a few tips for creating compelling and interesting content.

First, you'll want to have a strong introduction that sets expectations for your video and familiarizes new viewers with you and your content. You'll also want to cut out any unnecessary or filler content you can from your video. Combine footage wherever possible. If you're showing a craft, such as painting or making something, it's best to speed up the video and add a voice-over to explain the process rather than taking hours to go over each point.

While filming, it's important to ask yourself if this is what you'd want to watch or be interested in. And, while you're filming, make sure you have good natural lighting. Without good lighting, it can make a video look cheaper or more unprofessional. Try facing a window with natural lighting if possible. And, as I stated before, you'll want to be sure that you have good audio. People won't want to watch your video if there's a bad sound.

Developing Your Channel

Once you've begun to actually make your videos, there are some other things you'll need to consider in order to grow and develop your new channel. Most people might believe that, in order to be successful as an influencer, you need to be smiling and bubbly for the camera all the time. However, people actually connect with more and enjoy videos from people who are showing their authentic selves. You should also actually enjoy the content you're making rather than turning it into a scheduled chore. If you aren't having fun, your viewers will be able to sense that even through their screens. The real magic happens when you start getting more comfortable in front of the camera and really feel like yourself.

One way to help your channel grow is by collaborating, much like what I suggested in our chapter on podcasts. And, like podcasts, you should really start thinking about collaborations early on. Making content with other channels is a great way to grow your audience.

However, for this to be successful, it needs to actually make sense to your audience. Viewers are smart and they'll be able to sense inauthenticity. It would be better to reach out to similar hosts and channels to create videos both of your audiences will enjoy. Audiences can get excited about meeting a new guest on a familiar platform, which could lead to potential new fans for your own channel.

Now, the biggest thing to understand about creating a YouTube channel is this; don't expect to get "YouTube rich" overnight. Sometimes it takes creators years before they make any real money from their videos, and it can be quite frustrating. Plus, it can be hard to stay motivated to spend years creating content without anything to show for it. But that doesn't mean you should give up. There are a few ways you can make some income just starting out, which we'll discuss later in this chapter. And, if you really enjoy making videos, you shouldn't let the fear of failure keep you from creating.

YouTube Analytics

After discussing different ways to grow your channel, you'll need to understand how to actually measure this growth. Some people really love analyzing data, some might hate it. But no matter how you feel about it, YouTube analytics, and understanding the various different data it provides, can be extremely helpful. There are some metrics you'll want to pay attention to.

A click-through rate will tell you how enticing your titles are, and how clickable your thumbnails are. You can check the click-through rate for your channel as a whole or for each individual video you want to test. The rates vary with every creator, so establish your own benchmark to meet or exceed as you'd like. You can determine your goals by checking your current click-through rate, whether it's two, four, six, or eight percent. Try to improve these numbers by at least two or three percent in a year (Marshall 2021).

Another metric you'll want to keep an eye on is your watch time. The more watch time you get, the more YouTube will promote your feed. But that doesn't mean you have to create longer videos. You just need to maximize the value of your time. Look at your video's audience retention and compare it to others. However, if your average view duration is 60%-80%, then you're doing pretty well.

You can also measure your channel's growth by viewing your typical performance, how your latest video compares to your channel's average performance, your reach, which gives you a summary of how your audience is discovering your channel, and your engagement, which tells you how long your audience is watching your videos—sort of like your watch time. By keeping track of these numbers, you'll be able to note what tactics are working for you, what type of videos your audience prefers, and how to make future goals when it comes to developing your channel further.

Ways to Earn Money from Your Channel

Once you start to grow your channel, there are various ways you can make some extra cash. If your channel grows to over 1,000 subscribers and you've accumulated 4,000 hours of watch time within the last twelve months, you can apply to join the YouTube Partner Program (YPP) and monetize your videos directly (Freeman-Powell 2021). If you become a part of their program, you could earn money every time someone views your video, or any time ads are played. You'll also receive money for anyone who subscribes to a premium subscription with YouTube.

But, even before you reach that point, you can monetize your videos in various other ways, especially if you're just starting out. There are really a lot of different options you can explore, similar to what I've discussed in previous chapters such as reviewing products, using affiliate links, finding sponsors, and so on. Whatever route you choose, just remember to be fully transparent with your audience that you're partaking in paid promotions.

Content Marketing

As impossible as it sounds, the average person is exposed to 4,000 to 10,000 advertisements each day ("How To Craft Compelling Calls-To-Action | Co-Communications" 2021). With those kinds of numbers, it might seem daunting to make your own lasting impact, doesn't it? Not to worry. There's still hope. With content marketing, and if it's done correctly, you can produce a much higher ROI than traditional forms of marketing (Freeman-Powell 2021). This can be super effective, plus it can be fun!

But what is content marketing? Content marketing is where you give away videos, blogs, or other forms of content for free to your viewers or subscribers. Some examples of content marketing are blogs, YouTube videos, and podcasts. Creating a channel can give you an edge in the marketing field, making you stand out from competitors.

When you give away your content for free, you can possibly encourage a better relationship between you and your viewers. Those viewers are then more likely to become paying customers later on or will want to help you financially in some way or another. Plus, if your content is good enough, your viewers will start to share it and effectively market your brand...for free.

The better your content is, the more likely you'll be able to grow an audience. YouTube is so widespread that, if you continue posting great content, then you'll be able to gain a ton of subscribers in no time. And, the more your viewers engage with your videos, the more YouTube will promote your feed.

Join the YouTube Partner Program

The Youtube Partner Program is how regular Youtubers get access to special features. You don't have to be a partner to make some extra cash, but it sure does make it easier. Partners don't just have access to special video ads, but you can also earn money from having subscriptions for your channel and sell merchandise straight through YouTube itself.

To join, you'll need a minimum of 1,000 subscribers plus 4,000 hours in the last year. Then, you'll want to create an AdSense account. If you're planning to, or already are earning money on YouTube, you'll need to connect an approved AdSense account. Once you create an AdSense account, you just link it to your official YouTube channel.

Each monetization channel in this program has slightly different eligibility requirements. With the ad revenue option, in order to earn money, you must be at least 18 years of age. Your content must also be appropriate for ads. If a YouTube Premium member watches your videos, you can earn some money from their subscription plan, which comes automatically with being part of the YPP. Another way you can gain subscription fees is by having channel memberships. But, in order to sell channel memberships to your subscribers, you need to have more than 30,000 subscribers to your channel. Same with the merchandise shelf—you'll also need to be 18 years old and have at least 10,000 subscribers.

Sell Your Own Merch

Though you have to have a significant amount of subscribers to sell merchandise through YouTube, that doesn't mean you can't sell your own on your website or other platforms. Setting up an e-commerce store on your website is easy enough and can be super beneficial. Selling merchandise is meant to help represent you. This means your merchandise has to be unique and related to your brand.

You can sell anything from mugs to t-shirts, pillows to yoga mats. All you need is a manufacturer, supplier, or wholesaler to make and deliver your products. Some suppliers will deliver it straight to you, however, the best thing to do is to find a good print-on-demand company—one that will create and distribute your merchandise for you without the hassle of you figuring it out for yourself.

Some of the best print-on-demand sites include Printify, Printful, and Spring. These types of websites already have a variety of products that you can simply place your designs on, or create designs using their templates. Then, you link these shops to your website's e-commerce stores and that's that! Your viewers can purchase directly from your website's store, pay, and the company will make and ship their purchase straight to them.

Sponsors & Affiliates

Like with websites, blogs, or podcasts, you could also look into using affiliate links or sponsorships to earn some extra cash with your videos. Affiliate marketing can be used when you're just starting out. You can encourage your audience to visit whatever brand you've chosen to be affiliated with. You will then earn some money made through your— you guessed it — custom link. We went over affiliate links in the first few chapters, and you can find information about sponsorships in the podcast chapter.

These are just a few ways you can begin to monetize your YouTube channel, even if you don't have a large follower base just yet. If creating videos is a passion of yours, keep working at it until you reach your goals. This could be a great way to make some extra cash, or even turn it into a full-time job as a YouTube influencer! Just remember, YouTube won't help you make money fast, and it does take a while to build an audience. However, if you keep at it, you could turn your hobby or passion into a lucrative asset.

8

ONLINE SURVEYS

TAKING ONLINE PAID surveys is another unconventional job that doesn't pay an hourly wage, but could be a great way of earning money online in your spare time. While you won't get rich quick, you can make a little extra cash by taking these online surveys. Legitimate ways to make money from home, while wearing those comfy pajamas and eating pizza, are few and far between, surveys can give you that extra spending money you might want during these tough times, and even later on.

Thousands of companies are looking for feedback on their products, services, or ideas from random, and potential, consumers. While it won't make you rich, it can give you some extra spending money while putting in very little effort.

Taking paid surveys is easy and could definitely be done from anywhere at all as long as you have good internet. They could even be done on your commute to and from work (if you aren't driving, of course), or in those moments right before bedtime when you have some extra hours to spare. Most survey sites are free and require no education or skill, so anyone can do it. And, depending on the website, surveys can be fairly simple, albeit a bit dull sometimes.

Some sites will pay more than others, and most will disclose the cash value for each survey. However, you'll want to avoid the websites that compensate their survey takers in confusing point systems. To get started, all you need to do is sign up on survey sites. You might need to confirm your email address before getting started as well. After signing up, you'll receive notifications whenever a company is looking for people to take their survey. Most websites, however, will require you to meet a certain pay threshold in order to start withdrawing money or before you can request a payout.

Are Surveys Worth It?

No matter what site you go with, the earnings from taking surveys could be meager compared to other work opportunities. Also, you might have to work extremely long hours just to reach their pay threshold, which is sometimes as low as $5. In addition to your time, you'll need to give up valuable personal data to these third-party survey sites. Sometimes they will ask you for more personal information such as your birthday, your address, how much money you make per year, any health problems, your family history, and other such information that might make you feel uncomfortable to give out. The biggest risk with taking online surveys is that you aren't able to find out how your data is going to be used. You'll be putting yourself out there at the mercy of other websites and companies.

Even with these drawbacks, some people might still consider taking surveys as an attractive option. After all, there really aren't any barriers when it comes to taking them and they can be done anywhere at any time. However, there are some tips I would like to note if you plan on taking online surveys.

First, don't over-share. It might seem obvious, but if you're asked to give out your Social Security number, any information about your personal bank number, driver's license, or any other personal card, you probably shouldn't do the survey. These questions are extremely intrusive and this data could be used to steal your identity. Second, you should create an email specifically for taking surveys. Most survey sites will send you several emails a day and this way you can keep your main email clutter-free. If you do want to take online surveys, consider downloading anti-malware software. This can keep your computer or other electronic devices free of viruses and other problems third-party sites might have. You'll want to protect your computer and other devices from these viruses.

Now that you know a little more about surveys, let's dive into what websites you can sign up with to start making some extra cash.

Branded Surveys

Branded Surveys is a website that collaborates with market research and Fortune 500 companies to pay consumers to take their surveys. They will then use these surveys to improve their marketing and products. After completing surveys, you can redeem points for money, gift cards, or donate to some charities, if that's what you prefer.

This website has a 4.3-star rating on Trustpilot, with many excellent reviews (Robinson 2021). However, common complaints about this site include that surveys are often filled up too quickly, and many people actually get kicked out of surveys about halfway through. Some people have also complained about not receiving the right amount of points once they complete a survey, and that there are some problems with prompt payments. However, despite these complaints, Branded Surveys is still considered a legitimate company.

After setting up an account with them, you can log into your dashboard to see what surveys you qualify for. These are listed under the Spotlight label. You can also see how much time it will take you to finish, plus how much money you can make. Keep in mind that this time is an estimation and won't tell you exactly how much time you'll spend on these surveys. Besides viewing the different surveys from your profile, you can also choose to receive email notifications. However, you'll need to be able to respond to these notifications quickly as they tend to fill up.

Branded Surveys also has a bonus program with three tiers: Bronze, Silver, and Gold (Robinson 2021). Your status will then influence how many bonus points you can earn. For example, Bronze members can earn a specific percentage of completing surveys in a certain amount of days. If you're in the Gold tier, this percentage will increase. You'll then receive these bonuses each week.

Once you've accumulated the number of points needed, you can cash out by either selecting cash or exchange your points for various different gift cards. Or, again, you can opt for making a donation to certain charities they support. You will usually receive your gift cards within just a few days.

Swagbucks

If you've been looking at online surveys to make more money, then you've probably already heard about this site. But they're actually much more than just surveys. You can earn money from simply shopping online at various stores, watching other peoples' videos or ads, looking something up on the web, or answering surveys--there are a lot of different ways to earn money. Swagbucks also offers gift cards to those who have finally reached the minimum payment threshold on their site or you can receive money through your PayPal account.

This site offers opportunities for surveys, but many people have found they're disqualified most of the time. Swagbucks aggregates third-party surveys, so some sites it sends you to are better than others (McMullen, Delfino and Ramirez 2021). They will send you to other websites that are partnered with them. And, through their in-depth profile survey, they try to match you to surveys that will fit your specific demographic. However, as we said, the disqualification rate can be high, and since you'll be going through other websites, you'll need to put in your information on each site. Plus, like with other survey sites, it will take you a while to earn enough points.

The minimum age requirement for Swagbucks is 14 years old with adult supervision. The payment threshold for this site is fairly low at just $5 and, if you don't want to receive gift cards, they send this money directly to your PayPal account. The conversion rate for Swagbucks is comparable to other sites. For most rewards, one point is worth one cent, although Swagbucks does offer some discounts on certain rewards, which can bring the value of these points to about ten cents (McMullen, Delfino and Ramirez 2021).

OneOpinion

If you've tried out online surveys before, you might know that it can be a frustrating cycle. You can get disqualified from a survey before you even get to finish it, and then only make about fifty cents at the end. However, it's a little easier with this site. Like Swagbucks, OneOpinion also uses an in-depth personal survey to match your demographics and uses third-party sites.

Compared to other sites, OneOpinion will give you the opportunity to take surveys that you actually might qualify for, which means you can earn more money for the time you actually spend taking the survey. However, the one downside to this survey site is the number of points you'll need to accumulate before you can cash out.

Like with Swagbucks, OneOpinion will have you enter basic information about yourself before asking two more questions. Some of these questions won't be too difficult--they just want to make sure you're actually focused, though some will be assessing your qualifications for the different surveys. This site is well-known for matching their survey-takers to surveys they can actually qualify for. And, they still give you 500 points for each of the first five surveys you're disqualified from. Even if you aren't disqualified, sometimes they will give you those 500 points simply because the survey you were going to take was already filled up. However, it is slightly more difficult in reaching that payment threshold in order to redeem your points for rewards.

This site has a $25 threshold, which is higher than some other survey sites. Points are basically worth about a tenth of a cent each. Some people might earn around $2 per hour they spend taking surveys and that's about it. While OneOpinion makes it easier to take surveys and has a lower disqualification rate, it can be difficult to make money.

Survey Junkies

Like OneOpinion, Survey Junkies also has a high threshold for redeeming points. However, this site's effectively-vetted surveys, easy-to-use dashboard, and uncomplicated reward system do make it easier for those who want to take their surveys. Survey Junkies feels more like an aggregator than an actual survey site, which means they use third parties to dole out their surveys.

They include an extensive profile survey that helps match you to the surveys you'd be more qualified to take and offers 25 points upfront simply for signing up. They also offer 50 points for answering their first survey, which simply wants to know certain personal information about your demographics...But, even with this demographic survey, and because Survey Junkies sends you to third-party websites, you'll most likely have to repeat the process of putting in your information over and over again.

While it's easier to earn points on Survey Junkies than it is on other sites, actually getting the rewards can be a bit more difficult. You'll need to reach 1,000 points, or $10, to hit that payment threshold in order to redeem or cash out. When you do actually go to redeem your points, the site will ask you for your address in order to verify your identity, which some people might be hesitant to do. Once you give them your address, you'll be able to redeem your points without any trouble.

Opinion Outpost

Some surveys might overwhelm survey-takers with various different survey opportunities or spans, however, Opinion Outpost doesn't. With this site, you will enable you to easily take surveys without much effort. As a beginner, you might appreciate their straightforward point system as well, which also works out to be around ten centers per point. Opinion Outpost is considered one of the better survey options out there because of this.

Once you've finished signing up, you can see your dashboard where you'll be able to view your points and your personal information. Their dashboard is simpler compared to others, which will make it easier for you to locate everything you need. At the top of your dashboard, you'll simply find one button that says 'Take a Survey,' and that's how you can access their extensive list of surveys to complete.

Before you can start completing surveys, however, you'll need to complete some short questions. According to them, these questions will help create a better survey-taking experience and to increase your chances of earning more rewards. These questions will vary each time but you might see some repeats. After, you'll be matched to surveys which will again tell you how much you can earn and how much time it will take.

When you finally have enough points, you can redeem them in several different ways. Like with most sites, you can cash out with PayPal and Amazon. However, this site also gives you the choice to earn MileagePlus miles as well. You could also enter into raffles for drawings up to ten thousand dollars, or make donations to a charity.

Toluna

Unlike many other sites, Toluna allows survey-takers to choose specific topics for their surveys, such as gaming or other categories. However, they are considered to have one of the lowest pay when it comes to taking surveys. With Toluna, there are two different types of surveys to complete.

First, you'll need to fill in profile surveys so the site will be able to send you surveys you might qualify for. For example, if you answer that you have an iPhone in one of these profile surveys, Toluna probably won't give you any surveys where you will need to be an Android user to qualify. The longer surveys are where you can choose the topics you want to answer questions about. All you need to do is pick a topic and Toluna will send you to an available survey. Between the survey center and their numerous emails, you'll have plenty of opportunities to start with what seems like endless longer surveys.

The good thing about Toluna is that they will let you know immediately if you're disqualified from a survey as soon as you click on it. On other sites, you might waste some time answering questions before being disqualified. But, as a consolation for being disqualified, Toluna does enter you into their monthly sweepstakes to earn a chance at winning some money.

You can either cash out with PayPal or even receive a check in the mail, something not many other sites offer. However, their rewards aren't that cheap. If you choose to receive a physical check, Amazon gift card, or cash via PayPal, the conversion rate is about $1 USD per 3,000 points. If you reach 500 points, you're entered into their monthly $4,500 USD drawing, with 1,000 points giving you an opportunity to win an LED TV.

They also have another unique option. Instead of choosing the above payouts, you could choose to buy yourself, or a friend, a virtual present. These are called "Gifties" and could include a leaf blower, a DIY cheese-making kit, and a variety of other gift cards. Each Giftie costs between 50 to 500 points. However, these are more like raffles where you can earn the chance to win the real objects, rather than actually receiving them.

Taking surveys online might not be the best option if you're looking to make some big bucks. However, they're extremely easy to do, can be accessed basically anywhere as long as you have the internet, and can bring in some extra spending money. It's easy work. You might actually enjoy taking these surveys, which might lessen the feeling of it being an actual job.

9

PHOTOGRAPHY

IF YOU'VE EVER HELD an interest in photography, or perhaps even selling your photos, then now would be a great time to learn more about how you can actually do that. Whether you've gone pro, or just take photos with your smartphone, photography could actually be a good source of income if you actually spend time researching and improving your knowledge and skills.

Whatever your level might be, there are a growing number of ways you can monetize the photos you've already taken or are going to take. And, there are numerous ways you can develop your photography skills from selling your Instagram stock to making photo books. In this chapter, we'll cover what equipment you can use, how to sell your photos online, and even how to take this hobby into being a full-time freelance photographer.

Essential Equipment

Before you can start uploading your work online, you need to understand that, the better equipment you have, the more likely your photos will sell. Now, this doesn't mean you have to have the most expensive camera out there. In fact, you can simply purchase the cheapest DSLR camera and work with that. Once you've got that DSLR, you can begin looking into selling your photos online through various different ways such as stock libraries, prints, or other such products.

DSLR, or digital single-lens reflex, cameras will produce higher-resolution images you'll need to create high-quality prints. Your iPhone or Android might seem to take amazing photos, but their image resolution won't be high enough to print. If you try, your images will come out looking grainy or pixelated if a client tries to print the image in a bigger size.

When you have a good camera, the next thing you'll need is good photo-editing software. Adobe Lightroom and Photoshop are probably the best options for editing your photos, but they might be a little pricey and need a subscription. There are some free software and applications you can use such as FastStone Image Viewer, which can open RAW files straight from your digital camera and save them as JPEG, TIFF, or PNGs—the most used formats for uploading photos to websites. This application does pretty well with basic edits such as color correction, straightening or cropping, and contrast.

Raw Therapee is sort of like Lightroom, with a bunch of tools for fixing colors, contrast, and more, while PIXLR is very similar to Photoshop. They even have some of the same shortcuts, and you can use PIXLR straight from a browser or from their app for free. There are also some phone apps you can use such as Snapseed.

However, if you're serious about photography, I would highly recommend paying for Adobe Lightroom or Photoshop and learning how to use them. Tons of photographers sell, or give out for free, something called a preset which can make editing even easier and faster. They act as filters on Instagram, though you can tweak them to fit your own style more in-depth if you're experienced enough.

Stock Libraries

Stock libraries, such as Getty Images, Dreamstine, or Shutterstock are just one way you can sell your photos online. Photographers can upload their images to these sites and earn a percentage of their image sales each time. Some sites will require you to submit your work so they can review the quality before you can join their programs. And, even after that, some sites will continue to review all of your submissions. You should consistently be reviewing the quality of your work. You shouldn't get too discouraged if you are rejected—there are still a ton of sites that might accept your work.

Alamy

When you first get into selling your photos online, I would recommend checking out Alamy. Students are able to make one hundred percent of the sale for up to two years. On average, the images on Alamy sell for about $80 USD, but your photos could sell from anywhere between $20 to $500 USD, depending on what your images will be used for. However, if you aren't a student at a university, this won't really work out for you.

Non-students will typically get 50% for images that are exclusive to Alamy, meaning you aren't selling these images on any other stock library websites, with non-exclusive images receiving slightly less. You can also sell phone pictures through their Stockimo app where you can earn a 20% cut from your uploaded photos.

Dreamstime

Dreamstime is another stock image library that will offer over 50% of the sale to their exclusive contributors. This site is one of the more well-known sites for buying and selling images online. The price of your images will also increase depending on the number of times it is downloaded by customers. So, the more your image is downloaded, the more you can make. New images can sell for around $0.34 to $5 USD. If you're wanting to sell photos taken on your phone, you can start with their free Dreamstime app for Android or iPhone.

Getty Images

Getty Images is another well-known site for buying and selling photos. They usually pay 15%, but like with many other sites, they offer even more if you agree to become their exclusive contributor. Meaning, you won't sell your image to any other image-selling websites. Single images on Getty Images cost about $70 to purchase, but the type of license or subscription plan a customer buys will determine your final pay per image.

Shutterstock

Even if you've never sold or bought photos online before, you've probably heard of Shutterstock. The amount you earn per photo also depends on the license or subscription a customer buys, like Getty Images, and it also depends on your lifetime earnings with them. At first, you'll only be able to earn about 15%, like with most other sites. But, the more you are able to sell each year, the more you'll earn. However, they reset your earning potential each year, which means you'll be starting over every twelve months.

Tips to Make Extra Money Selling Stock Photos

The best tip for selling photos online is to upload your best photos to multiple stock libraries. It's also worthy to note that you'll want to try and include people in your photos, though you'll need a model release form for your subjects to sign. Usually, stock libraries will have templates you can print, sign, and submit.

Before you start selling your images, check the Terms and Conditions. This is very important as it will give you all the necessary information you'll need including how much you'll be paid, and when. They will also tell you what happens to your work if you decide to delete your account with them later.

To maximize the chances of your photos being seen, and downloaded, you'll want to use relevant keywords when uploading your photos. This metadata will help make it easier for potential customers to find your photos with only a few simple words in the search engine of the library.

Selling Your Photos as Prints

If you're hoping to sell physical prints of your images, it's very important to use a proper printing lab. Simply printing from home won't cut it. But don't worry, you'll still have loads of freedom in selling photo prints from labs. You'll have all the creative control you want. You get to decide your subjects, style, who you want to sell your prints to, and you'll have full control over overpricing.

To start, you'll need to find a good website that will be able to quickly upload high-resolution images for your customers to view. You don't want your portfolio or shop to have low-quality images, so finding a high-end website host is a must. These hosting sites will even handle the actual printing and any postage whenever you make a sale.

However, there is a catch. Many of these sites will charge for hosting your site and they take a cut from each sale you make. Some good websites to check out would be Zenfolio or Smugmug. If you don't really like the idea of sharing the profit, you could set up your own eCommerce store on any website hosting site and use print-on-demand places, which we'll cover next.

Print-On-Demand Products

Making prints or gifts to sell on your own can be pretty straightforward. The best choice is to find a print-on-demand website where you won't actually have to purchase any prints or products yourself, but will instead make the items once someone orders them.

Print-on-demand won't just give you a way to offer prints or wall art, but you could also offer even more products such as rugs, mugs, and other house decors. The best thing about this route is that they will make the products when someone places an order, rather than beforehand. So you won't actually need to spend your own money buying stock. Plus, these companies will do all the heavy lifting for you. They make, print, and ship the orders for you, so all you need to worry about is uploading your images or designs.

One such print-on-demand company is CafePress. It's completely free to set up and run a store through their site. Your royalties might vary, based on retail prices, discounts, or promotional prices, but overall, you can make some good money from selling their various different products. Zazzle is another company that will allow you to set your own royalty rates between 5% to 99%. However, you don't want to set that percentage too high, as it will be added to the overall price and might make your products a bit too expensive for customers to buy. So, the higher the percentage, the more your products and prints will cost.

Redbubble is one of the more popular sites where photographers and creators alike go to sell their images and designs. Redbubble will provide you with a basic amount to start with, and you can set your earning percentage to around 20%, though you can change that if you wish. Your images will be placed on their various different products like prints, clothing, and house decor, which makes it easier for you to sell your images. However, they have implemented a new threshold of about $21 USD so you can only cash in on your earnings if you make that much per month.

Another way you can sell your images is by using Instagram. If you don't like any of the above options, you can check out websites I mentioned before such as Printify, Printful, or Spring, and link their e-commerce stores to your social media or own website. After setting up your own store, and having some products on it, I would suggest buying some samples of these products (which they allow you to do at a cheaper price), taking some snazzy product images, and marketing them on your social media platforms. Instagram is a great tool to use, especially now that they have a products tab where you can link the images you post to your website store.

Becoming a Freelance Photographer

If you try out photography and learn you actually love taking photos, you could turn this hobby into an actual career. There are so many different niches in photography that could earn you some money: family photography, lifestyle, branding, wedding, and engagement, or anything to do with services many people and companies might need.

Like with all the other ways of earning money in this book, you'll need to figure out your niche. Maybe you really love animals. You could turn that love for animals into an animal portrait business. Or, perhaps you really love weddings. The wedding photography industry is actually super lucrative. Couples will pay thousands and thousands of dollars for a professional wedding photographer.

Once you find your niche, you'll need to work out your rate. If you're just beginning, I honestly would suggest working for free until you can build a portfolio and develop your skills. When you do finally start charging, you need to take into account your costs and time spent. You will need to pay for a business license, such as an

LLC, and will probably want to invest in getting insurance for your photography equipment. To figure out how much you should charge, you need to take all that into account plus your travel time, shooting time, editing time, and if you're paying any third-party websites to deliver your photos, you'll need to count that as well.

Now that you have a portfolio and have figured out your pricing, you need to market yourself. Fill your social media accounts with all of your best-quality photos, letting people know when you're available, and how they can get in touch with you. You can even get a bit creative and take some promo shots of brand products and tag them in your photos to get noticed if you're into product photography.

Despite the advancement in smartphone cameras, and the fact that many people think they can become professional photographers using their phones, actually becoming a freelance photographer is a lot harder than you'd think. The income, while it can be great, is often unpredictable, and you'll need a lot of patience, perseverance, and some talent to build your photography business. If you're a beginner photographer, I would highly suggest investing in some classes or online courses that can teach you more about how to work your camera, take better photos, and how to build your photography business.

Bonus Tips

When looking into using photography as a way to make more money, here are some things you should keep in mind. First, carry your camera everywhere! You'll never know when you'll go somewhere special or find something unique. Plus, this will give you the practice you'll need to hone your talent and skill as a photographer. You should also look into taking various workshops or photography classes. You'll always want to be developing your knowledge and skills if you're planning on making this into a life-long career.

Also: backup your photos! You'd be surprised by how often photographers will lose all of their hard work from faulty hardware or unforeseen malfunctions. Invest in one or even two external hard drives and keep your work on those. That way, if your computer crashes, you won't lose all of your hard work. This is very important and many beginner photographers might not even think to do this. So, stay ahead of the game and look into backing up your images regularly on multiple different devices.

And, lastly, don't just recreate generic photos you see over and over again online. Try to find your own photography style. This could include anything from the types of objects or people you photograph, to your editing style. Whatever it is—make it uniquely yours! Many photographers will create their own presets or find certain styles of shooting where their clients can easily recognize their work without even looking at the name. This will take time and effort, so don't feel too stressed if you don't find your style right away.

FINAL WORDS

The start of the COVID-19 pandemic caused a lot of people to wonder where their futures might be going. Through job loss and hours spent in lockdown, some might have even considered trying out different ways to make cash while waiting for their lives to return to normal. If you've picked up this book, this was probably you.

Maybe you've been let go from a job you've had for years, or perhaps you've been temporarily laid off. You might have been stressing about how to pay your bills, or have started to wonder where your life might be heading. Perhaps COVID has actually helped you realize that you've been neglecting hobbies or interests that have made your life just a tad bit brighter.

But the onslaught of this virus doesn't have to keep you from doing what you love. Being stuck inside doesn't mean that your life has to be put on hold until things go back to the way they were before. It just means that, now, you have the time to discover new things—especially different ways in which you can earn extra money.

After reading, you have some pretty good ideas to get you started to branch out in the different ways you could make money while staying at home. Whether you want to start a blog and earn money through affiliate links or write a book, start a podcast or sell some of your creative work online, this book has given you a basis on which to leap off of towards creating more sources of income for you to benefit from.

We discussed how to create and complete various jobs, some that could even be turned into part-time work when COVID finally eases up. You've learned about online teaching, and the potential it has to bring in extra money each month. You've learned how affiliate links work and how much you could make simply by creating a blog and engaging with your followers. We went over writing, creating, and recording books—something many people say they want to do but never had the time to actually do it. We even covered how some of these work-from-home solutions could turn into full-time careers such as becoming an English teacher abroad or starting up your own freelance photography business.

Some of these small jobs and hobbies have assisted me in creating extra income during COVID, and I hope that these ideas will help you as well. If not, you could use these as a basic idea of what you'd like to do anyway. Either way, this book has provided the necessary information you need to get started on working towards more passive and active income you can rely on even when you're stuck inside.

Plus, you might have discovered some new things about yourself you might never have known before. Maybe you've discovered that you're a writer at heart, whether you've developed a love for blogging, vlogging, or writing actual books. Maybe you've learned how much you love creating podcast episodes or that you're a pretty good photographer who could make money selling photos. Whatever your newfound hobby or love might be, you now have the tools to begin a new path, a new career, and even a new life, one filled with opportunities you actually enjoy.

REFERENCES

Bennett, Bo. 2021. "How To Make An Audio Book: A Do-It-Yourself Guide". Ebookit.Com.

https://www.ebookit.com/tools/bg/Bo/eBookIt/ucHgoPMz/How-To-Make-An-Audio-Book--A-Do-It-Yourself-Guide.

Collins, Bryan. 2021. "How To Make An Audiobook In 10 Simple Steps (2021)". *Become A Writer*

Today.   https://becomeawritertoday.com/how-to-make-an-audiobook/.

"Cuddle Clones Affiliate". 2021. *Web.Archive.Org*.

https://web.archive.org/web/20210123140633/https://affko.com/listing/cuddle-clones-affiliate/.

Cyr, Dannielle. 2021. "How To Craft Compelling Calls-To-Action | Co-Communications".

Co-Communications.

https://cocommunications.com/commentary/how-to-craft-compelling-calls-to-action.

Freeman-Powell, Paul. 2021. "5 Reasons Why You Should Start A Youtube Channel For Your

Business - Innobella Media". Innobella Media.

https://www.innobellamedia.uk/blog/5-reasons-start-youtube-channel-business/.

Galea, L., 2021. *What are the Basic Requirements to Teach English Online?*. [online]

Internationalteflacademy.com. Available at:

<https://www.internationalteflacademy.com/blog/basic-requirements-to-teach-english-online

> [Accessed 26 September 2021].

Hamilton, Jason. 2021. "How To Make An Audiobook: Publishing On ACX And Audiobook

Marketing". Kindlepreneur.   https://kindlepreneur.com/how-to-make-an-audiobook/.

Hayes, M., 2021. *What Is Affiliate Marketing? Your 2021 Guide to Getting Started*. [online]

Shopify. Available at: <https://www.shopify.com/blog/affiliate-marketing> [Accessed 28

September 2021].

"How To Make Money From Pet Blogging: Adsense Case Study 2021". 2021.

Bloggerspassion.Com.   https://bloggerspassion.com/make-money-from-pet-blogging/.

Marshall, Carla. 2021. "How To Start A Youtube Channel: 10 Brilliant Tips". Vidiq.

https://vidiq.com/blog/post/how-to-start-youtube-channel-10-brilliant-tips/.

Omukhango, Muthoni. 2021. "The Future Of Books – Ebooks – Reflections By Muthoni

Omukhango". Web.Archive.Org.

https://web.archive.org/web/20210304223950/https://muthoniomukhango.kenyaclc.org/the-future-of-books-ebooks/.

Sabatier, Grant. 2021. "16 Legit Surveys For Money Sites". *Millennial Money*.

https://millennialmoney.com/best-survey-sites/.

Saurina, Antoni. 2021. "How To Join The Youtube Partner Program, And Boost Your Corporate

Channel". *Wearemarketing.Com.*

https://www.wearemarketing.com/blog/how-to-join-youtube-partner-program.html.

Sheehy, Kelsey. 2021. "How To Make Money From Your Podcast - Nerdwallet". Nerdwallet.

https://www.nerdwallet.com/article/finance/4-ways-to-make-money-from-your-podcast.

"Thinking Of Starting A Podcast? Here Are 7 Things To Know - RSS.Com Podcasting". 2021.

RSS.Com Podcasting. https://rss.com/blog/thinking-of-starting-a-podcast.